T0339498

# Judgment

Judgment is simple, right? This book begs to differ. Written for all students of the law—from undergraduate to supreme court justice—it opens the reader to a broad landscape of ideas surrounding common law judgment. Short and accessible, it touches upon many pathways that lead out from the phenomenon of judgment in common law jurisdictions. This book is unique in its brevity and scope. It not only engages with the core operation of judgment as legal decision but considers questions of authority and reason and broader issues of interpretation, rhetoric, and judicial improvisation. The aim of this book is not to present a summary of research or a comprehensive 'theory' of judgment, nor is it bounded by the divisions of different legal subjects. Instead, it is a handbook or companion for students of the law to read and return to in their studious journeys across all common law topic areas, providing readers with a robust and open-ended set of tools, combined with selected further readings, to facilitate their own discovery, exploration, and critical analysis of the rich tapestry of common law judgment.

**Thomas Giddens** is senior lecturer in law at the University of Dundee, Scotland. He founded the Graphic Justice Research Alliance and is the author of *On Comics and Legal Aesthetics: Multimodality and the Haunted Mask of Knowing*, editor of *Graphic Justice: Intersections of Comics and Law*, and coeditor of *Law and Justice in Japanese Popular Culture: From Crime Fighting Robots to Duelling Pocket Monsters*. His research focuses on critical, comics, and cultural legal studies, with particular interests in aesthetics, epistemology, and visuality.

**Part of the New Trajectories in Law Series**

Series editors
Adam Gearey, *Birkbeck College, University of London*
Colin Perrin, *Commissioning Editor, Routledge*

for information about the series and details of previous and forthcoming titles, see www.routledge.com/New-Trajectories-in-Law/book-series/NTL

A GlassHouse Book

# Judgment
New Trajectories in Law

**Thomas Giddens**

Routledge
Taylor & Francis Group
a GlassHouse Book

First published 2022
by Routledge
4 Park Square, Milton Park, Abingdon, Oxon OX14 4RN

and by Routledge
605 Third Avenue, New York, NY 10158

A GlassHouse Book

*Routledge is an imprint of the Taylor & Francis Group, an informa business*

*British Library Cataloguing-in-Publication Data*
A catalogue record for this book is available from the British Library

*Library of Congress Cataloging-in-Publication Data*
A catalog record for this book has been requested

ISBN: 978-0-367-33363-8 (hbk)
ISBN: 978-1-032-25384-8 (pbk)
ISBN: 978-0-429-32978-4 (ebk)

DOI: 10.4324/9780429329784

Typeset in Times New Roman
by Apex CoVantage, LLC

'But we're all walking in the night, now, on ground we don't know.'

—Ursula K Le Guin, *The Books of Earthsea*
(Orion 2018) 846

# Contents

# Acknowledgements

This book is intended as an entry into the rich tapestry of ideas related to common law judgment. It is the product of a range of reflections and avenues of research I have taken so far in my career and seeks to be reflective of the open expanse of legal study and research beyond what is typically taught on undergraduate law degrees and in core foundation modules. It is aimed at all students of the law—from undergraduate to supreme court justice—who wish to get a better understanding of judgment and open themselves to its vast and irresolute complexities.

The book was written across a period of great personal and professional change. It spans a shift in institution, a shift in residential location to the other end of the United Kingdom, and all the attendant variations in life that come with such large-scale upheavals. It is perhaps fitting, then, that the work you are entering is a restless one: it does not seek to provide answers or resolve tensions, but instead asks and embraces questions and the uncertainty of whether or not they might have answers. This underlying ethos is not just a symptom of my recent peripatetic existence but is also key to understanding judgment (and law more generally), which far from representing certainty and order is characterised by the complex and never-ending navigation of the vicissitudes of life and the human condition.

In the production of this text, there are many unacknowledged authors—including people like Helen, Arthur, Jasper, David, Rachel, Luke, another David, a certain Andreas, Sarah, a couple of Colins, Tim, Karen, Peter, and so on. In the spirit of uncertainty, I will not try to resolve that list. Instead, I will simply thank a limited number of those who were most closely connected to the manuscript.

Thanks, then, to Brian Christopher Jones, Nicola Tulley, and Sean Whittaker, for using some of whatever time they had to look at a draft manuscript for this book and offer insightful and helpful comments. Also, to the stalwart Colin Perrin for his editorial mastery. And particular thanks, also, to one Adam Gearey, not only for his vision in instituting this series of excellent and accessible texts, but for seeing some promise in my perhaps reckless idea of trying to write a book on judgment that is less than 50,000 words long, and also for casting his learned gaze over a draft.

Despite such inputs, all the failings and limitations of the output are of my own making.

# Judgment as . . .

Judgment is simple, right? Undertaken by the judiciary and written into law reports, judgments form a key part of the everyday activities of those who study and work with the law. For lawyers, judges, and other students of the law, these recorded decisions are commonplace and are used and applied, read and analysed, as one of the core resources of the law. We access them via online databases, download them, read summaries of them, pick out the important bits, and reduce them to single principles, material facts, and abbreviated names. *Woolin, Wednesbury, Woolmington*—and many others. They become shorthand for the principles and doctrines of the common law.

A judgment is a *judgment*: it's what the court says; it's the authoritative statement of the law, of how we should interpret an established principle or a piece of legislation. A judgment is objective, rational, neutral, unbiased—and, therefore, just.

Right?

This book is about exploring judgment in a variety of ways. It does not seek to build a 'theory' of judgment, if such a thing is even possible, but instead presents a brief collection of different perspectives or models of how judgment might be understood. The aim is also to transcend the some-what artificially separated 'foundation' subjects of law since judgment is something that occurs, or that is used, in all areas of law.

Indeed, what makes a judgment 'law'? A judgment might be an object of legal study, something made by a judge, something that is recorded, edited, reported, and put into an online database. But it might also be a way of thinking, a method for resolving conflicts and uncertainties. Of dealing with the unexpected troubles and vicissitudes of communal life. But how does this work in law? How does 'legal' judgment relate to judgment understood more broadly, or vice versa?[1] What characterises the activities of judgment?

---

1 A note on spelling. I am using 'judgment', without an 'e', throughout this book. While 'judgement' is the UK English spelling of the word, and elsewhere I am using UK spellings

How is it done? What are its modes of operation? How central is this activity to the intellectual life of a lawyer, as an undergraduate student or practitioner or judge or armchair enthusiast? How does the way we conceive of what judgment is (as a document, as a statement of law, as an intellectual activity, as a process, as a somewhat arbitrary ending to what could be endless deliberation, as an interpretive practice) affect our understanding of law—as an ideal, as a set of general principles, as an institutional form, as a practical activity?

Importantly, this book does not try to recount or engage with the vast literature and discourse on judgment (although the further reading may lead intrepid readers further into the complexities of that realm). The intent is merely to gesture towards ways of thinking about the nature of judgment in law from a range of perspectives. To this end, we will try to avoid delving into the rabbit holes of particular viewpoints and endless citations, although there are some writers whose work is worth dwelling on a little, and we will do that a few times across the book.

If you were to imagine the words 'Judgment as . . .' ahead of each of the chapter titles, it would go some way to capturing the book's approach. In what follows, we will trace together a number of different models of judgment. These models are not complete or uncontested, nor are they mutually exclusive: they are contingent, and they overlap and intersect in different ways. This book does not try to resolve or explore all of these interactions, but it does indicate some of them. The purpose is not to give a single 'answer' to the question 'what is judgment?' (probably an impossible task), but rather to open readers up to a range of possible ways of understanding the complexities involved in—and involved in understanding—legal judgment. And, more specifically, judgment within the tradition of the Western common law.[2]

In doing this, it is hoped that some of the ways in which judgment underpins and shapes the common law in general will be indicated, alongside an

---

of words as opposed to their US or other variants, I have adopted the exclusive use of 'judgment' because I am writing in an expressly legal context, and 'judgment' is the preferred spelling in legal contexts—whether one is using US or UK English. Note, though, that there may be instances where we are talking about 'judgement' more broadly (albeit perhaps not explicitly). But because it would not be possible to determine with certainty which context we are talking about at each use of the term, and because using 'judg(e)ment' would get tedious, for ease I will use 'judgment' throughout.

2 Other traditions, such as the civil law, Eastern jurisdictions, and indigenous legalities, also involve their own questions of judgment, but they are sadly beyond the limited scope of this book. Having said that, some differentiation from the civil law tradition will be noted in places, given its shared European history with the common law, and we will also make some acknowledgement of the common law's underlying imperialism.

appreciation of how thinking openly and broadly about legal judgment can invigorate and develop our understanding of law and our ability to work with legal materials and ideas. Moreover, this can happen not only through the intricacies of particular doctrines and legal categories, but by engaging with some of law's 'big questions' on a more general level through judgment itself: What is law? What is justice? How is authority legitimate? Where does it come from? Why does law have power in society? How do we determine what a law means?

Through the lens of judgment, this book embodies a key lesson that students of the law should appreciate wherever they can. Working with the law is not about learning answers and memorising doctrines or sets of rules; instead, it is about engaging in a way of thinking, a way of processing individual conduct, communal relations, and social life. And armed with such an understanding, the intricacies of specific laws and doctrines can be understood and worked with in a more meaningful, skilful, and critical manner.

To engage with law is to engage in judgment: to navigate the contingency, constructions, and uncertainty of law's norms, principles, doctrines, and texts, and their application to specific sets of circumstances. Law is never set or certain or simply 'there' to be found—it must always be produced through judgment. But judgment can take many forms and be understood in many different ways. This book works to open doors to some of those ways and, it is hoped, by doing so, will enable readers to take their own steps beyond and pursue some of the intersecting 'models' of judgment that this book gestures towards.

# 1 Legal decision

A judgment is a legal decision. It is the words or outcome given by a judge in a particular case. It supposedly signifies the end or resolution of that case. In this sense, a judgment is an ending; it draws a line under the dispute or question at issue so everyone can move on. This is perhaps the most common-sense understanding of judgment on a practical level, particularly for lawyers and other students of the law. A judgment is the decision in a legal case, which (if significant) is then reported and compiled with other judgments into law reports. Before we move to think about some other understandings of judgment in subsequent chapters, it is important to dwell in a little detail on this 'standard' model of judgment for law.

We will begin by considering the ways in which judgment operates as a resolution to individual disputes (section 1.1) before considering how this process results in the general principles of the common law in the doctrine of precedent (section 1.2) and, eventually, the general emergence of the common law that derives from the accumulation of individual decisions (section 1.3). Along the way, we will also note how the idea of judgment as legal decision opens up to some of the multiple perspectives explored in later chapters.

## 1.1 Resolution

Judgments draw proceedings to a close, end disputes, bind parties, hold villains to account. While appeals may take place, these avenues eventually run out (either with the highest court in a jurisdiction or with an international court, such as the European Court of Human Rights), and a final judgment will be given. Indeed, most cases do not appeal, and the judgment at first instance is also the final one. This 'final' quality of judgment is part of its practical function in a legal system. It also leads to questions about the authority of judgment, as well as concerns about justice, the role of the legal system, and the values or ideals that underpin that system. The question

DOI: 10.4324/9780429329784-1

of authority has its own chapter (see Chapter 2), so in this section we will instead focus briefly on the role of resolution within the legal institution and as part of its wider social context of operation.

One way to think about the nature of judgment as resolution is to consider the distinction between vengeance and retribution. This is quite a well-trodden area of debate (we will discuss it some more in Chapter 2), but it illustrates something of the institutional nature of a legal decision and how this can break cycles of disagreement between parties.

Most disputes do not end up in court with a legal judgment to resolve them. Things can be settled informally (one way or another) between the parties concerned, or soft-law options can also be used, such as mediation or arbitration. Resorting to a judicial court to resolve a dispute, to attempt to right a wrong or achieve some sense of just closure, is often the last resort. Indeed, this is how courts seek to position themselves so they are not overburdened. And, in many cases, the threat of court proceedings can be enough to get things sorted without a court ever being involved (for example, the threat of a lawsuit might stop a party from continuing to breach a contract or ensure an organisation provides adequate safety procedures for their products and services).

A judgment issued from the legal system—perhaps more so if included in a law report—can thus have various effects, both specific to a case and also to society more widely. For particular cases, a judgment ideally acknowledges the grievances of each party involved and provides a practical solution, be it the redistribution of loss through compensation, prescriptions for parties to behave in a particular way (e.g. to adhere to a contract or maintain the status quo), or the imposition of punitive measures (e.g. punishment for crime, which is a dispute between the state and an individual). There may also be some direction given on possible policy changes that would affect parties beyond those involved in the case being decided. But for the individual parties, it is the words of the judgment—backed up by state or legal authority (see Chapter 2)—that arguably enable law to have its effects.

More broadly, having recourse to this method of solving disputes may also serve to reduce a culture's reliance on methods of revenge and violence and, as mentioned above, can serve as a 'guarantee' for softer options, such as arbitration, that can be backed up by court involvement if their outcomes are breached. It is by instituting an authoritative mode of adjudication that the legal system short-circuits interpersonal disputes or harmful retaliation. A judgment represents the official statement of the parties' rights and relations and so ends the matter at hand and draws the dispute to a close. Moreover, it does this by positioning the giving of such judgments as unbiased: that is, as fair, just, and reasonable as between specific parties (e.g. citizen and citizen in civil cases or citizen and state in criminal ones) and thus as authoritative, binding, and legitimate. In the adversarial systems that are characteristic of the common law, the court has hearings—it listens to each side of the story, each gets their 'day in court'—and it makes a balanced and unbiased judgment in relation to them. This fairness may (also) be determined in relation to wider and often somewhat amorphous concerns of public policy.

This may be a relatively familiar or instinctive notion of judgment. It does not guarantee, however, that parties will be satisfied with the outcome or agree that it is just or that the decision is actually neutral or unbiased in all senses—the existence of appeals and critical discourses of the media, politics, and legal studies are testament to that, not to mention the vagaries of moral philosophy.

Indeed, it is important to note that law is not simple and clear-cut and is actually inherently uncertain and requires analysis and construction to establish its principles and meaning. If law had correct answers that could be easily discovered, there would be no need for lawyers, judges, or courts at all. This feature of law thus means there is arguably always a deeper question over what ideals or values the legal institution instils through its ongoing processes of judgment. These questions include concerns over how these processes operate and the sources, grounding, and limits of their authority. Resolving disputes between specific parties is far from everything that judgment is and far from everything that it involves—as we will explore together across this book.

## 1.2 Precedent

Even as a legal decision, judgment already has more than one meaning. It is both the actual decision in the specific case—a resolution, if you will—and the record of that decision that is disseminated and used by lawyers and academics in later cases and analyses. As a verb, a court passes judgment in a case; as a noun, a judgment is an object to be used in subsequent argumentation.

In these two perspectives, we can see something else about legal decisions. Not only is any specific case decided, but that decision is then enshrined or stored in some kind of archive to guide or limit future decisions in similar cases. This is known as *stare decisis*, or letting the decision stand: in order to produce justice, we should treat 'like cases alike'. In other words, if a series of events takes place and a judgment is rendered in relation to it, if that same series of events takes place again, it stands to reason (see Chapter 3 on reason) that the same judgment should be made again. The same pattern of facts should produce the same legal decision, the same judgment. In this sense, then, a judgment becomes a piece of law, binding on future cases that are sufficiently 'similar'.

Judgments as objects in this sense, as 'nouns', are really just shorthand for the 'verb' of judgment—a claim that the same outcome would be produced in similar circumstances. Over the centuries of common law, this notion of *stare decisis* results in the emergence of relatively stable principles and doctrines. Think, for example, of the offence of murder, which has no statutory basis in England and Wales but is defined only through the judgments of the courts. In many ways, the doctrine of *stare decisis* is a foundational aspect of common law systems and is characteristic of the common law method. Ironically, it did not exist in the early years of the common law, but it became established practice around the 17th century and has enabled decisions to build up into an archive that can guide decisions in future cases.

Part of the logic of *stare decisis* is the extraction of a general rule or principle from a particular decision—that is, the 'law' of the case, which then applies to other similar cases. Often courts will seek to do this in order to test the validity of their decisions (this is especially so in higher appeal courts). However, if this process simply involves the mechanical application of like cases to like cases, it is not necessarily logical or just and can instead be seen as actually *lacking* any process of judgment at all:

> Precedent without . . . reasoned discourse . . . tells us what has been done in the past but such a statement of past occurrence is not an argument or reason, it has no greater normative status than any other anecdote or repetition of times past.[1]

The doctrine of precedent, of *stare decisis*, is not simply a requirement for future courts to automatically apply the outcomes of previous decisions in similar cases, but is the enshrining of a particular decision that will become part of the body of (authoritative) legal resources. This collection of preceding law then needs to be judged as appropriate and relevant when considered in future cases. Put simply, the question is one of determining when and in what way cases might be 'distinguished' from previous cases. Put with more complexity, it is necessary to reflect upon (interpret, deliberate, contextualise) established principles as an integral part of their application or use. This can be seen most clearly in the critical study of law, which involves questioning sources as they are used or, for example, in the

---

1 Peter Goodrich, 'Critical Legal Studies in England: Prospective Histories' (1992) 12 Oxford Journal of Legal Studies 195, 208.

development of more general principles by higher courts as they interrogate how preceding decisions apply more widely.

In short, applying previous judgments involves making judgments: about the relevance of that preceding decision; about how the principles, discussions, and facts in that previous decision should be interpreted; and about institutional legal questions on the authority and cogency of that previous decision and its suitability to the present case or to the present social or political context. Precedent is not simply followed but must always be read and applied in the context of the current case—even if this may not be acknowledged in the written record of a judgment.

## 1.3 Common law

The building up of precedent results from a central principle of the common law: that like cases should be treated alike, that decisions should be allowed to stand. Over the centuries of legal decision-making, a complex body of law has developed based upon the judgments of the judiciary. Given the complexity of this body of law, it is debatable whether its whole content can ever be known, let alone comprehensively analysed and applied to a new case. The common law is an unwieldy mass that is vastly complex and is distinct from the relative neatness of statutory or codified law that is laid down by a parliament or legislature.

Statutory law, or statute law, is not the product of judicial decision-making but is the outcome of a particular bureaucratic or parliamentary process. Laws are proposed—not necessarily with any pre-existing formal law in place—and are then debated, drafted, amended, and finally passed into force. This is quite different from the discursive or argumentative process of judgment that draws its substance from rules and principles that are seen to already be in existence as binding in the archive of the common law. However, their distinction is not so clear cut. Statutory law does often build upon or attempt to codify common law decisions, and—more importantly— the application of this statutory law is filtered through the judicial process. Judgments are regularly passed on the interpretation, meaning, and scope of statutory provisions. Controversial, but one might even go so far as to say that statutory law only gains its full legal meaning within a common law jurisdiction once it has been authoritatively read in a judgment that determines its meaning. In this way, even statutory law is absorbed into common law processes of judgment.

From the intricacies of individual cases recorded across centuries of history, the common law has emerged as a particular method of legal resolution. It is a method that is characterised not by codified rules but by the qualitative principle that is evidenced through specific decisions. It is the slow burn of this case-by-case resolution that, over time, accumulates into the body of principles we call the common law. There are distinctions to be made between this style of legal adjudication and other judicial systems—most notably the civil law systems that rely more heavily on codified rules. In historical versions of the common law, in contrast, the legitimacy of common law decision-making stems not from anything inherent in the form or process of judgment itself or from the authoritative nature of the 'source' of a codified law, but simply from the traditional quality of the common law as a way of doing things. We will consider the authority of judicial decisions more fully in the next chapter, but here it is valuable to preliminarily sketch out this vision of the traditional sources of the common law.

The idea goes like this: the common law is law not because it decides anything in particular or follows particular formal procedures but simply because it has a history that stems back to time out of mind. What this vision of the common law tradition overlooks is the influence of a wider range of external factors on its development, including the scholarly and civil law practices of continental Europe (we will discuss some of this more in Chapter 3). Roman law, for instance, is widely regarded as one of the first fully fledged codified (written) legal systems—the *Corpus Iuris Civilis* of Justinian was claimed to be the entirety of the law and needed only to be applied to the case at hand to find a legal resolution of a dispute. While the common law did not adopt the same degree of codification, in its early days it did share many practices with the Roman tradition—most notably, the reliance on text and written forms of law (in writs, as well as recorded judgments), as well as the practical reliance on the scholarly expertise of the Church in administering these texts.

The common law has a deep temporal structure, existing not as a static code to be read and applied to each new case independently but as an ever-evolving sea of doctrines that mediates a range of political and social influences across history. Understanding judgment as legal decision involves an appreciation for the effects of this understanding. In an instant sense, a judgment resolves a dispute, but when framed in light of the idea that decisions are only fair if they are consistent—that like cases be treated alike—what emerges over time is a fully fledged body of law to be drawn from in each new case.

Tradition is thus an appropriate word for the common law, given its links with the word 'translation'. With each new case, each new decision, the previous law is recalled, examined, discussed, and applied—it is translated from the previous contexts of decision to the present one. Each new case updates the law, translating the past into the present. As we will encounter in later chapters (notably Chapters 5, 6, and 7), the written form of the common law that has emerged has a significant part to play in enabling previous decisions to be communicated for use in future cases and to be communicated to future generations of judges and lawyers.

The primary means by which this takes place is via law reporting. Most cases—while operating within the common law tradition of judgment—do not amend or update or clarify the law but apply it to resolve that specific case. In these instances, the aspect of legal decision in play is primarily the resolution of the individual dispute, although done in light of more generally established principles that are read and applied. The judgments that are encountered in databases and law report volumes are not just the transcripts of each and every judgment. Courts themselves keep records of these transcripts and have done so for centuries. What law reports consist of are cases that have some significance for the development of the common law.

Where decisions disrupt or develop the body of the common law in some (minor or major) way, the larger temporal structure of the common law is also engaged. Thus, where a judgment changes or sets a new precedent or clarifies or develops the understanding of an existing doctrine or principle, that case is deemed worthy of reporting: it is important enough to record in a more accessible way than court transcripts. Law reports are edited and compiled, with significant metadata and additional information included alongside the judicial reasoning itself (typically in the form of case headnotes). These documents are compiled into law report volumes, constituting a printed—and more recently digital—database of legal decisions. It is these law reports that are relied upon most centrally by lawyers, academics, judges, and other students of the law for analysis, study, and decision-making (see also Chapter 8 on questions of audience).

This practical structure reflects the conceptual structure of the common law: in the court transcript can be seen the idea of legal decision for individual parties, while in law reports we find the common law as a body of established principle to be read and applied in future cases. But this practical arrangement is also the product of judgments over which cases are worthy of reporting. Only some precedents are reported, but all decisions carry that same authority. Any particular judgment, then, is always both an instant decision and enduring precedent.

This unresolved tension is a phenomenon that is characteristic of the idea that like cases be treated alike. This is a principle that seeks to ensure fairness and justice of the law through a method of deciding specific cases in light of preceding similar cases rather than through the reading and application of a codified law or judges 'making it up as they go along' (although see Chapter 9 on improvisation). While *stare decisis* seeks to authorise legal decisions, this method of authorisation remains questionable. For example: what authorises the judiciary to develop the common law in the first place? How is 'similarity' established in an authoritative or just way? What makes judicial readings of the common law authoritative? It is to such questions of judgment as authority that the next chapter turns.

## 1.4 Further reading

* For various materials and guides relating to the practice of law reporting, see the website of the Incorporated Council of Law Reporting for England and Wales: <www.iclr.co.uk/knowledge/>
* For a detailed analysis of the emergence of the written common law, and in comparison with other systems in Europe, see John P Dawson, *The Oracles of the Law* (University of Michigan Press 1968).
* A shorter discussion of the emergence of precedent can be found in Ian Williams, 'Early-Modern Judges and the Practice of Precedent' in Joshua Getzler and Paul Brand (eds), *Judges and Judging in the History of the Common Law and Civil Law: From Antiquity to Modern Times* (Cambridge University Press 2012).
* For further discussion on statutory and common law, see Patrick S Atiya, 'Common Law and Statute Law' (1985) 48 Modern Law Review 1.
* For a general discussion of the nature of common law judgment, in particular its distinction from political judgment (e.g. of the legislature in making statutory law), see Graham Mayeda, 'Uncommonly Common: The Nature of Common Law Judgment' (2006) 19 Canadian Journal of Law and Jurisprudence 107.
* A more advanced discussion of the *continuity* of legal judgment with judgments in art and aesthetics, despite institutional law's general claim that legal judgment is distinct from such frivolous concerns, can be found in Costas Douzinas, 'Sublime Law: On Legal and Aesthetic Judgements' (2008) 14 Parallax 18.

# 2 Authority

Judgment is authority. Such a claim, at least initially, involves two things—roughly mapping onto the noun and verb understandings of judgment mentioned in the previous chapter. As a noun, judgment is *an* authority, something to be used to give authority to an argument. As a verb, it is an *exercise of* authority, something that is done with and through authority. Let us elaborate on these dual aspects further.

A judgment is passed down by a court as *an* authority—a piece of law, a nugget of authorised text—that can be deployed and utilised in legal and academic argument. 'Cite some authority', a tutor might say in essay feedback, or 'What do the authorities say about this?'—and a judge on the bench would likely expect the same from the advocates appearing before her, just as practitioners and academics alike come to expect judges to cite authorities as objects or resources to help elaborate and justify their decisions.

The other dimension of judgment as authority is closely related to this but involves thinking a little further about the authoritative nature of judicial decision: judgment is an *exercise of* authority on the part of the judge and the state bureaucracy of which they are a part. This is judgment as a verb but also as a noun: it is due to this *exercise of* authority that a judgment becomes *an* authority (because the 'noun' judgment is really just shorthand for the 'verb', as noted in Chapter 1).

Understanding judgment, then, involves understanding questions of the legitimacy of legal authority and its relationship with other forms of judgment. What distinguishes judicial opinions from other kinds of opinion? Where does legal authority come from? To approach aspects of these admittedly very big questions, we will consider the legitimacy of judgment (section 2.1) before reflecting a little on the nature of the office of judge that enables 'authoritative' judgments to be made (section 2.2) and ultimately considering the potential (lack of) underlying authority for the state that underpins the institution of law in general (section 2.3).

DOI: 10.4324/9780429329784-2

## 2.1 Legitimacy

Judgments arguably have authority because they are legitimate, yet there are many ways in which a judgment might be considered legitimate—for example, because they are well-reasoned or follow particular procedures in the way their decisions are made. These factors can be said to be 'internal' to the judgment—they are factors that can be seen within the judgment or decision itself, in the way it is put together or the way it expresses its argument. We shall discuss these aspects in more detail in the next chapter (see Chapter 3). These aspects are important but arguably do not in themselves satisfy an attempt to legitimate legal decisions. For example, a shopkeeper or office worker—or indeed a law student drafting an essay or an advocate submitting an outline case—might be able to put together a well-reasoned argument and analysis that could fulfil these 'internal' requirements. But that does not mean they are legally binding in the same way they would be if a member of the judiciary made the same decision using the same sources and lines of reasoning. The question for the current chapter, then, relates to the 'external' aspects of judgment that can be seen to enable the content of judicial decisions to become authoritative.

To begin this questioning, it is worth spending a little time reflecting on how or why 'everyday' opinions might be different from judicial ones—and whether this distinction makes sense or is in any way 'natural' or objectively true. One way to do this is to think about two potential reactions to being wronged—vengeance and justice—which are also raised in Chapter 1. How does something personal like 'revenge' differ from an institutional reaction that might be said to produce 'justice'? How or why is 'revenge' different from 'justice'? In examining this question, we will encounter a possible distinction between mere opinion and legitimate legal decision.

A key feature of vengeance is an emotional or personal reaction to being wronged. Revenge involves feeling subjectively wronged and then acting to harm the party who has wronged you. This can be captured in the idea of 'an eye for an eye', which operates on this logic of paying back a harm done. In a sense, this arguably achieves justice. The party who has been wronged gets to pay back that wrong, acting out their injustice in a way that redresses the balance between the parties. If I steal your car, it seems fair that you might steal something of mine of equal value—a car for a car, for example. There is certainly a logic of justice at work here. Why, then, might we need to institute a different logic of justice? Why do we need to have judges and laws if we can simply seek revenge under the balance and proportionality of an eye for an eye?

One issue with 'an eye for an eye' logic is how we value things. If I steal your car, and you steal mine in retaliation, this only works if the cars are of equal value (and, of course, that you have the capacity and opportunity to steal my car). An easy way to do this might be to look at the commercial or financial value of the two cars in the current market; if one car is worth more than the other, then the difference might need to be made up by other objects being taken or by money. Is this still revenge? It might be the case that you care more deeply about your car than I do mine, regardless of their financial value. How do we quantify that sentiment in order to balance the scales of 'an eye for an eye'? There is a question about fairness here. On a superficial level, 'an eye for an eye' seems fair, but it almost instantly becomes very difficult to achieve fairness in practice because everything has a different value, and this value might vary between parties even for the same object or conduct.

In order to counteract this potential for a lack of fairness, the institutional form of laws and courts operates to standardise certain values and to administer them in a consistent way across different cases—to treat, you might say, 'like cases alike'. Indeed, this is much of what was discussed in Chapter 1 around the idea of precedent in the common law, with *stare decisis* insisting that previous decisions must stand and be applied to future decisions in similar cases. This *institution* of justice—rather than justice as the vengeful activities of private parties—can be understood as an attempt to legitimate the process of resolving disputes in society on a wide scale. It has various effects, and looking at the simple differences between personal vengeance and institutional judgment can indicate some of the key features of the supposed legitimacy of judicial decision-making.

The most overt distinction is that personal vengeance is individual while institutional judgment is public or communal in nature. Revenge tends to be fuelled exclusively by personal interests, operating only in relation to rectifying the harm that was done on a personal or individual level, with no concern for others in the community. Institutional judgment, on the other hand, is always concerned with both the individual parties and the wider community. This is part of the logic of precedent: if the decision should be allowed to stand, if like cases are treated alike, then any future case will potentially fall within the ruling of any previous case, and thus each and every decision necessarily affects the whole community. All members are thereby treated 'fairly' with respect to the same conduct. In order to ensure this measure of fairness is enabled, judgments must be communicated publicly—and this is done via law reports, as was outlined in the previous chapter. Institutional judgments are thus public in two senses: in the sense that they speak the community or bind the whole community and in the sense that they are recorded in a publicly accessible form or communicated to community members (see Chapters 5, 6, 7, and 8 for more on judgment's textual form and its communication).

Other distinctions that might be noted between vengeance and legal judgment include the emotional quality of vengeance. Vengeance seeks a visceral, emotionally satisfying outcome, while judgment is more measured. What does 'measured' mean? Typically, this can be understood as reasoned or carefully considered: in navigating the complexities of valuation and fairness, legal judgments claim their legitimacy not in arbitrarily asserting balance or fairness but through carefully explored reasoning and analysis of the common law, of preceding decisions, of public policy, of the effects on the parties, and of possible future cases. This is the territory that we will explore in the next chapter—relating to the internal rationality of judgment that operates to secure its supposedly authoritative or legitimate status. But for our present concerns, this measured or reasoned quality of judgment can be contrasted with the individual and emotional quality of vengeance.

The lack of reason in vengeance, its typically emotional quality, risks spilling over into an outcome that is not proportionate, that is not 'an eye for an eye' but is instead an emotional release in the interests of the wronged party only, with insufficient concern for the interests of the other party or the wider community. The claim of law is that by being rational, the subjective bias that comes with emotional engagement is diffused or avoided (we discuss emotion and irrationality more in the next chapter too). The rational logic and formal structures of institutional judgment suppress emotion and operate to deliver a fairer justice that—as noted above—works at the level of the community as well as that of the individual parties. By resolving disputes through the legal institution, through the bureaucratic administration of reasoned decisions, a logic of justice is followed that aims to be fair for everyone.

We might connect this to the idea of the rule of law—that no one is above the law or that the law binds everyone, not just specific parties, and thus takes a generalised form. From our discussion so far, it can be seen that this idea of general laws being applicable to all derives from the intricacies of specific cases and disputes being resolved in a way that takes communal fairness into account, not just the parties in an individual case. And importantly, that it is this structure—characteristic of the common law—that arguably makes judgments legitimate.

## 2.2 Office

Within the legal institution, these legitimate judgments are not proffered by just anybody—but by those qualified to do so. That is, by those authorised by the legal system itself. Something of the self-sustaining or self-authorising quality of law can be seen here (see section 2.3), but in terms of the present section, it is the office of the judge that is important. Part of what makes legal decisions authoritative is that they cannot be produced by just anyone, but only by those people who occupy the office of the judge. One important question, of course, is who gets to occupy that office and why—but more importantly for our present discussion, why does the official nature of judgment make a difference in terms of the authority of the decisions given?[1]

To occupy an office is to take on a public function. An office holder is no longer an individual, no longer a mere mortal, but is imbued with the power and authority of the institution of which the office is a part. For example, when someone takes up employment at a government department answering customer service queries, they are fulfilling a function for the state as well as representing the state to the people who contact them. Part of that person's conduct is not their own—it is the conduct of the state. Similarly, the conduct of people who hold other public offices—politicians, police officers, and so on—is not just the conduct of private individuals but becomes the conduct of the institution of the state.

Ultimately, this division between public and private aspects of an office holder results in a splitting of the person into two dimensions, as can most clearly be seen in relation to the monarch or sovereign of a nation. On one level, the king or queen of a country is an eating, sleeping, aging, fallible human being—like us all. On another, she (although traditionally he) is the incarnation of the endless line of monarchs of which she is but one part, hence the phrase 'The Queen is dead. Long live the Queen!' The human body dies, but the monarch, the sovereign—the office—does not. This phenomenon of the sovereign's 'two bodies' (one mortal, one mystical) filters down to those who hold public office, including judges.[2] The people who sit on the bench are not just people, but are expressions of the common law, of state authority and legal rule. It is this 'official' status that renders the words of judges different from those of other people—and different from the personal opinions of judges when they are not at work.

---

1 Office is intimately connected with jurisdiction. There is a lamination of different jurisdictions of office within most common law systems. For example, 'higher' level judges supposedly wield greater authority, and different judicial roles can preside over different areas of the law. The co-existence of plural systems of law within a single territory, such as sharia law, canon law, indigenous law, or some international instruments, add further complication to this. We will not engage with these jurisdictional complexities, but they are worth noting. For a fuller engagement with jurisdiction in general, see Shaunnagh Dorsett and Shaun McVeigh, *Jurisdiction* (Routledge 2012).

2 Even this is not a static or 'natural' division since the 'mystical' body can be interpreted in line with a range of different ideologies or political preferences. Karl Shoemaker, '*The King's Two Bodies* as Lamentation' (2017) 13 Law, Culture and the Humanities 24, listed in the 'Further reading' section for this chapter, explores this in more detail.

Accordingly, holding judicial office entails certain responsibilities, as does reading and studying the words expressed through the authority of that office. The words of jurists are not to be taken lightly. On one level, this is merely practical: judgments are, in practice, binding and have real effects in society (regardless of whether we understand why that might be or if that binding quality is legitimate). Reading and understanding these texts is thus not only important but has an ethical quality in relation to the ongoing practice and development of the common law and the effects its decisions have across society. As Olivia Barr elaborates:

> Taking up the office of jurist . . . requires attending to and taking respon-sibility for the practice of the common law tradition, which requires an ability to converse in the languages of common law, including the idiom of precedent and the language of procedure . . . the jurist now has a responsibility to attend to the technical and material forms of com-mon law practice as a way of accounting for the creation and conduct of lawful relations.[3]

The judgments of the legal institution have constitutive effects in society: they define and regulate relations between people in society, thereby pro-ducing what Barr terms 'lawful relations' in the above quotation.

It is perhaps a common instinct to think of individuals' relationship with law as one of, for example, master and servant, or a parent disciplining a child: it is a relationship where punishment is always a threat or conduct is always manipulated or encouraged in some way. But this model is quite nar-row; taking a broader perspective on the institutional role of law in society, its effects relate not simply to punishment and rehabilitation but to the rela-tionships between members of the social community in general. Contrac-tual relations, interpersonal relations (where harm is caused, where families break down, etc.), relations where property is bought and sold and occupied, or the making of communal decisions about how to administer the country in its best interests (e.g. elections). It is the place of the legal institution—and thus of judgment, not just as legal decision but as binding authority—to oversee and facilitate these relations, as the arbiter of last resort.

This function, as we saw in Chapter 1, operates because judgment is widely understood as a means of resolution—of ending disputes between individuals, one way or another. The status of the judge as an office is important in this regard. As an office, a judge is not a private individual,

---

3  Olivia Barr, *A Jurisprudence of Movement: Common Law, Walking, Unsettling Place* (Rout-ledge 2016) 80.

not just your neighbour or someone down the pub or a talking head on a news programme, but a supposedly unbiased public figure. Judgments are not decisions of private individuals but of the authoritative body of the state. It is their public quality, the fact they are (ideally) interested in the general administration of society more than their own personal whims, that arguably helps to secure their status as expressions of authority. By being public, by being 'official' in all senses of the word, judgments transcend the interpersonal dispute they are dealing with and render a public statement of law. They state the lawful relations in a particular case and—as principles of law—of lawful relations in cases of that particular class in general.

Here we see judgment as authority in its sense as a noun: judgments become authorities in part because of their general applicability across a class or range of different concrete situations or 'cases'. Take the formation of a contract: thinking legally, it is not the law that Mr X has made an agreement with Ms Y to buy her collection of ferrets but that (depending on the jurisdiction) general principles of offer, acceptance, consideration, and the intention to be bound are present in the specific case of X and Y and the ferrets, and thus there is a contract. This general or abstract quality of law is part of its practical operation and way of seeking justice by establishing and developing general rules that apply to everyone. And this can also be seen in the structure of the office of judge, as an abstraction of the judging individual away from their 'human' form that turns them into an expression of generalised state authority.

## 2.3 Sovereignty

So judicial opinions are somehow different from everyday opinions—they become authorities because they are authoritative. But where, ultimately, does this authority come from? Why, other than its 'public' status or its general or abstract quality, is the office of a judge an authorised one? Being public may not be enough, as public or general decisions can still be made that have bad or harmful consequences for many people or still protect one set of interests more than another, or a decision may be 'public' in terms of the way it is made (by considering communal interests and so on) but nevertheless be made by someone who is not actually occupying the office of judge. If we follow this line of thought, it seems there must be something else that authorises judgment, that turns it from everyday opinion into legitimate legal authority.

We have seen that the official status of a judge plays some part in the authority of judgment. But there remains a question, not necessarily of what makes judgments authoritative *per se*, but of what authorises the office of the judge so its occupants can produce authoritative opinions. The question becomes, then, one about the legitimacy of state authority more generally—about the role of government and the politics of power. It is a question of the power that underpins or underwrites the words of judgment in general and thus renders them authoritative.

It is tempting to say that the words of judges are backed by a threat of violence from the state. And in some senses this is true, to the extent that we can say state authority is backed by violence. Indeed, violence can be seen in many areas of state security, such as the police and the armed forces, that expressly use physical violence in order to coerce or eliminate those who would threaten the public order. But in this we come up against the same question of authority: what (if anything) makes the violent activities of the state legitimate and the violent activities of, say, someone committing assault or murder or terrorist activities illegitimate?

In the context of judgment, the question is one of the sources of authority for the spoken and written words of a judge. In broader state security terms (which arguably the practical functioning of a judicial system rests upon), the question is the source of authority for violent state actions. In a meaningful sense, this is the same question: how are the activities of state governance (be it legal rule, police power, or military force) justified, authorised, or otherwise made legitimate? In the case of violent harm, this question becomes more poignant and more obviously difficult, but the complexities and difficulties also filter through to more 'peaceful' state activities, such as judicial interpretation. This is not just because the words of judges work their way through state bureaucracies to potentially produce violent sanctions,[4] but also because judicial reading and writing can itself be understood as a violent activity—a point we shall return to in more detail in Chapter 7 when we consider interpretation.

The key concept to be elaborated here is sovereignty. In thinking about questions of legitimate authority (e.g. of judgment) and its relationships with the people who are subject to that authority (i.e. citizens or members of society), the concept of sovereignty is very significant. Traditionally, the sovereign was the person who was in charge of a country or state—the monarch, the king or queen of a realm who often derived their authority from a divine source, claiming a divine right to rule. An early attempt to explain the legitimacy of the sovereign without simply relying on recourse to the divine was made by Thomas Hobbes.

Hobbes imagined a world without a state and assumed it would be full of violence and insecurity, a world in which everyone was free to violently take

---

4  For a detailed elaboration of this point, see Robert Cover, 'Violence and the Word' (1986) 95 Yale Law Review 1601, listed in the 'Further reading' for this chapter.

resources from each other—to enact personal vengeance, like that discussed above. Hobbes argued that we give up our freedoms (notably our freedom to be violent) to the sovereign. It is then the sovereign, instead of the people, who wields what becomes *legitimate* violence in order to provide protection and security for members of society. This is sometimes known as having the monopoly on violence: the sovereign is all-powerful, free to choose how to seek this protection by any means they choose within their jurisdiction.

The element of 'choice' in sovereignty is important. A later theory from Carl Schmitt focuses on precisely the capacity of the sovereign to choose and determine things: from the boundaries of the community to the rules within it, who is 'in' and 'out', and—most importantly for Schmitt—when the rules do not apply. For Schmitt, it is precisely this ability to suspend the rules—to decide upon when an 'exception' is permitted rather than holding the monopoly on violence *per se*—that renders an entity sovereign. Everyone else is simply subject to the rules; only the sovereign can suspend them.[5]

But still, the question remains: what authorises these decisions? The sovereign may indeed be the person who decides the exception or opts to use violence to protect its subjects, but why is their decision authorised? In many ways, we cannot ask such a question of the sovereign: they are defined precisely by their authoritative status, their ability to decide the limits and exceptions of the political order of life. The authority of the state comes not from anywhere but is inherent in its sovereignty, in its status as that which determines the boundaries of a political community. And here we see the importance of the interactions and relationships between the state and the individuals over which it casts its authority, over which the judiciary cast their decisions. For what is at stake is not only the tensions and disagreements over rights, duties, and interpersonal disputes, but the existence of individuals as political beings, as members of the community that is constituted by the rules of society as instituted in law—that is, their existence as legal subjects, as beings subject to the rules and (supposed) protections of law. It is sovereignty that determines whether you are 'in' or 'out' of the law.

In modern society, democratic systems seek to temper this extreme or ultimate form of sovereignty. One of the key examples that Giorgio Agamben discusses is that of the Nazi concentration camps: these camps are a site where individuals are stripped of their legal protection by sovereignty, and the power of the sovereign—to determine their fate, their membership or existence within the communal order, their status as human 'life', and so

---

5  See Carl Schmitt, *Political Theology: Four Chapters on the Concept of Sovereignty* (George Schwab tr, University of Chicago Press 2005). Schmitt's famous formulation is: 'Sovereign is he who decides on the exception' (5).

on—shines upon them unmediated by rights or any legal guarantees. But Agamben also warns that the widespread deployment of security and surveillance mechanisms means that this 'state of exception', as found in these camps, can potentially open up anywhere, anytime, in a modern democracy. And here we see again the question of legitimacy—when or why is it legitimate for a sovereign to decide exceptions in this way?

Framed more critically, it may be that violence is what defines justice. It is where violence becomes its most severe that 'justice' (i.e. state law) is able to emerge: it is the entity that is the most violent that is able to hold the position of sovereign and thus institute a state.[6] The difference between a terrorist, thug, or pirate on the one hand and a monarch or sovereign on the other is not anything inherent in the way they make decisions or exercise their will. Instead, it is simply that the sovereign is the one who has won—they represent the power or force in society that has defeated or is able to suppress the violence of others.

A pretty bleak vision. But what about the democratic processes we use to ensure a 'legitimate' government? Surely these save us from the violent imposition of an illegitimate authority? Such processes underwrite the authority of judicial decision in that laws are enacted by democratically elected parliamentarians, and judges operate and decide in relation to those laws. But this is problematic on at least two levels. Firstly, common law decision-making is not wholly bound to statutory legislation, with the emergence and continual development of common law doctrines and the operations of precedent being an overt site where judges, not the legislature or executive, make law (see Chapter 9). Secondly, and in tension with the first point, parliaments—despite the checks and balances of the separation of powers and the voice of the electorate—can, and have, enacted laws and provisions designed to enable the exposure of citizens to the 'pure' sovereign power of the state, with recent examples taking the form of increasingly rigorous security, surveillance, detention, and immigration controls as noted by Agamben.[7]

Going deeper, democratic processes are themselves instituted by the state—and thus paradoxically rely for their legitimacy as a process not on

---

6  Sovereignty is shot through with various paradoxes like this. Neal Curtis, 'Superheroes and the Contradiction of Sovereignty' (2013) 4 Journal of Graphic Novels and Comics 209, listed in the 'Further reading' section, is a good overview of these various tensions, demonstrated through examples from superhero narratives.

7  For a good introduction to Agamben's insights into this political exposure, see Amy O'Donoghue, 'Sovereign Exception: Notes on the Thought of Giorgio Agamben' (*Critical Legal Thinking*, 2 July 2015) <https://criticallegalthinking.com/2015/07/02/sovereign-exception-notes-on-the-thought-of-giorgio-agamben/>.

their 'natural' fairness but upon the authority of the state itself that they seem to make legitimate (for more on this, see Chapter 7). That is, the state as a democratic institution is authorised only by processes that it puts in place itself—and is in this way can be understood, paradoxically, as self-supporting or self-authorising.

So, and perhaps troublingly, we are left without a clear-cut source of authority for state power. The authoritative nature of the state, and thus of judgment as an official expression of the state, derives either from violent enforcement, from the democratic process that has no preceding authority, from a divine source that we are likely unable to categorically identify, or—perhaps most accurately—from the self-supporting power of sovereignty itself. An authority that imagines itself into existence and institutes post hoc processes (e.g. democracy) to seek its own legitimacy, but ultimately does not 'come from' anywhere at all.

## 2.4 Further reading

- On the 'two bodies' thesis (i.e. the division of the mystical and mortal bodies of the monarch), in particular exploring the way ideologies of state authority claim different versions of the 'mystical' body that authorises the law, see Karl Shoemaker, '*The Kings Two Bodies* as Lamentation' (2017) 13 Law, Culture and the Humanities 24.
- On the relationship between the words of judgment and the potential for violent state enforcement, see Robert Cover, 'Violence and the Word' (1986) 95 Yale Law Review 1601.
- For fuller engagement with the various paradoxes of sovereign power, discussed through superhero examples, see Neal Curtis, 'Superheroes and the Contradiction of Sovereignty' (2013) 4 Journal of Graphic Novels and Comics 209.
- For some discussion on the difference between revenge and justice, as well as some aspects of sovereignty and violence in general, see Thomas Giddens, 'Natural Law and Vengeance: Jurisprudence on the Streets of Gotham' (2015) 28 International Journal for the Semiotics of Law 765.
- An examination of the hierarchical quality of sovereignty and its 'escape' from the institution of the state can be found in James Martel, 'Why Does the State Keep Coming Back? Neoliberalism, the State and the Archeon' (2018) 29 Law and Critique 359.
- For some reflective commentary on 'office' in general (not just of judges—but including them), see Shaun McVeigh, 'Afterword: Office and the Conduct of the Minor Jurisprudent' (2015) 5 UC Irvine Law Review 499.

# 3 Reason

Judgment is reason. In the previous chapter, we explored a number of *external* factors in the question of judicial authority; in this chapter, we turn to consider some *internal* factors of judgment. Namely, we will examine how the particular structure and reasoning involved in making a judicial decision might help ensure it is authoritative or legitimate. In this sense, judgment can be understood as a particular form of reasoning. It is a mode of thinking or problem-solving that follows particular methods and approaches.

We will focus roughly on two questions. Firstly, why are rational methods adopted, or why are they seen to produce authoritative decisions? Secondly, what are the limits of reason and how does it relate to other influences on judicial outcomes? We will work our way through these issues, beginning with the type of reasoning involved in common law judgment (section 3.1) before considering its limits in relation to various elements that a reliance on particular forms of reasoning—or, indeed, reason in general—might overlook or make unavailable within a judgment (section 3.2). We will then explore the possible 'irrational' factors at play in judgment and their potential necessity for justice (section 3.3).

## 3.1 Method

A leading approach to understanding judgment, specifically the authority of judgments as law, is to ground their legality in their internal structure or method. We have already introduced the supposed 'common law method' of treating like cases alike—a method that aims at fairness across the slow burn of the common law (see Chapter 1). Here we consider more directly the intricacies of the way judgments can be seen to be structured or conceptually arranged—that is, the idea of judgment as a particular mode of reasoning, which follows a certain form or method of rational logic in order to ensure the justness of the decision.

DOI: 10.4324/9780429329784-3

As we've already noted, these internal features are never sufficient to explain the authority or existence of law since there is a difference between a decision made in judicial office compared to one made outside of that office—even where the same mode of reasoning is used and the same decision reached. But these internal features of reasoning are important to grasp as one of the dimensions of judgment. In this section, it is the method of legal reasoning that we are interested in. There are a lot of different theories and perspectives and models of how judges decide cases or what the nature of legal reasoning is, and we do not have space or time to consider them all. In the broad spirit of this book, then, we will instead briefly outline a limited set of leading examples.

We will start with Neil MacCormick, whose work develops a sophisticated model of the way judicial reasoning unfolds or the intellectual procedures through which a judge's decision (should) pass if it is to be legitimate. It's not possible to fully explain MacCormick's ideas here (see the 'Further reading' section for more resources), but a basic version would consist of three broad features of (proper) legal reasoning: that a decision is universalisable; that a decision takes into account its consequences; that a decision is coherent with the existing law.

These features are in many ways symptomatic of the common law method we have already mentioned in Chapter 1: to treat like cases alike. If cases are to be treated alike, then any single decision should aim to be applicable across other similar cases; hence, a properly reasoned decision would be universalisable in terms of applying universally to other cases sharing similar facts. This universalisability may not be absolute, it might turn out to be problematic or become outdated, but its form as a general ruling is nevertheless required. And this universalisability, moreover, leads to the second criterion of considering consequences, since *stare decisis* results in the development of general principles from individual cases:

> That judges pursue them under the constraint of universalizability entails indeed that their decisions must always be decisions of principle . . . [and] legal rights are consequential upon . . . the decisions of principle we make in law.[1]

Deciding cases in a universalisable way produces principles and enduring rights and duties. Accordingly, when properly reasoning through a

---

1 Neil MacCormick, *Rhetoric and the Rule of Law: A Theory of Legal Reasoning* (Oxford University Press 2005) 120.

decision, these consequences must be taken into account—not in terms of the effects of the particular decision (what will this decision mean for the parties to the case?) but in terms of the rights or duties being established—that is, the precedent being set. This, in turn, results in MacCormick's final broad requirement of coherence, whereby the fact that decisions also produce principle means that each decision should fit with established general principles, with these general principles being exemplified in the detail of specific rules. As he notes: 'relatively detailed rules will be arbitrary if they are not also instances of more general principles, fewer in number than the number of the detailed rules, and more general in their terms.'[2] It is because they are derived from general principles that detailed rules, and specific decisions, are not merely arbitrary, and are thus justified or legitimate.

Such rational methods of judging or of explaining a decision are a key feature in the common law. In many ways, the methods of legal decision-making are a form of scholarship that derives from traditional methods of study that emerged during the period of the Enlightenment (discussed more fully in the next section). This can be seen in another leading model of common law judgment, which focuses on interpretation. Ronald Dworkin's theory of justice-as-integrity seeks to describe an idealised method of reasoning that, like MacCormick's, explains or justifies the legitimacy or legality of judicial decisions. For Dworkin, the central activity involved in making judgments is interpreting the previous law that has already been established. In common law judgment, this primarily becomes the interpretation of the body of case law that precedes the present case: what cases in the archive of the common law are similar, and how should they be interpreted and applied to this present case?

Interpretation itself is an important issue (indeed, see Chapter 7), but for the purposes of understanding the idea of reasoning as a means of justifying decisions, the central method Dworkin describes involves synthesising the entire history of the common law in light of the best possible world that a rule's interpretation could produce. Dworkin captures this idealised mode of reasoning by inventing a super-powered judge of infinite intellectual capacity and patience: Judge Hercules. Only the mythic Judge Hercules is capable of undertaking the impossible task of reading, understanding, and applying the entire history of the common law and thus reaching a 'correct' judgment. Mere mortal judges can only aim at or approximate this goal by engaging with the history of case law practically available to them and maintaining integrity with that past while imagining the best possible future that their

2  MacCormick (n 1) 201.

decision could produce. As Dworkin frames it: 'Law's attitude is constructive: it aims, in the interpretive spirit, to lay principle over practice to show the best route to a better future, keeping right the faith with the past.'[3]

Dworkin's method is thus about building up from the minutiae of individual cases, amassed over the centuries, and resolving into over-arching rules and principles, framed by a desire for a better world. Because it is not possible on a practical level to access true objectivity or an absolute source of authority for law, the common law must instead be internally justified through a method that seeks to authorise its judgments in the long term. And for Dworkin, this method is through particular procedures of reasoning that aim to build general principles from specific cases, ensuring that like cases are treated alike. Indeed, the intellectual heritage of Dworkin's 'Herculean' method can be traced to a method known as Renaissance humanism—a mode of intellectual endeavour, prevalent in the period of the European Enlightenment, that was characterised by investment in philosophy, coherence of reasoning, reflective interpretation, and the integrity of treating like cases alike, all working up to general 'truths' from the details of specifics[4] (we will discuss this in more detail in the next section).

We have barely scratched the surface of the range of alternative approaches and variations in how the phenomenon of common law reasoning might be explained, but the point here is simply to observe that the particular ways in which judges reason and explain their decisions—the requirement for judgments to be given with reasons—are important in understanding judgment. Judgment, in this model, becomes a form of reasoning—a particular form that follows specific protocols of rational deduction and logic. Although there is wide debate on precisely what those protocols are, as we've seen, leading versions tend to claim they proceed from the underlying method of the common law of treating like cases alike as a way of ensuring fairness between similar cases. The ways of reasoning towards universalised, general principles, with integrity with the previously decided law, operate to ensure this takes place across the now vast and complex web of the common law. They work internal to judgment, ensuring that the way individual conflicts, tensions, and interests are resolved tends to adhere to the mode of justice embodied in the doctrine of precedent.

---

3 Ronald Dworkin, *Law's Empire* (Fontana 1986) 413.
4 For a fuller elaboration of this reading of Dworkin, including a succinct analysis of his model of judgment in general, see Mark D Walters, 'Legal Humanism and Law-as-Integrity' (2008) 67 Cambridge Law Journal 352, listed in the 'Further reading' section.

## 3.2 Limits

We have discussed some ideas around the methods used by common law judges in order to navigate the competing interests of individual parties and communal values, with these internal factors or approaches seen to be an important way in which legal decisions are legitimated or justified. But as with any method, the result of these formal procedures has limits. Under the idea of judgment as a form of reasoning, a central element that can be seen to limit any such model is, of course, reason itself. There are particular limitations that these models involve that do not encounter the limits of reason, but in this section, we will aim to focus on the more general limitations that all of these reason-based methods involve.

Any method always entails a limit. By choosing a particular way of doing things—be it deciding who should pay compensation for a particular harm or deciding which phone to buy—limits are imposed on the possible understandings or outcomes produced. The scientific method, for example, involves a particular set of assumptions around the way the world works, relying on the selective controlling of potentially influential factors, on repeatability, and on the possibility of an outcome being true or false. It is then argued that this set of assumptions—this method—produces outcomes that we can rely on as truth or fact (on 'truth', see Chapter 4, and on the rhetorical nature of knowledge, see Chapter 8). In common law judgment, the methods adopted—of reasoning, generalisation, abstraction of principle across similar cases—enable the production of certain outcomes: namely, a set of rules of a particular type or form that we call law.

As we have already seen, this kind of law, as well as being grounded in reasoned logic and administered under sovereign authority, is characterised by being general and abstract (because it must treat like cases alike). This abstraction is a product of the method of precedent, which can have limits in its ability to react to new kinds of cases or changes in social structure and value, in that judges may be stuck with an old law that is no longer fair or required in contemporary society. But the interpretive or reasoned nature of law can also mean it has the capacity to adapt to novel types of cases (on automating judgment, see Chapter 5; on interpretation, see Chapter 7; on the creativity of judgment, see Chapter 9). But as indicated above, there are also deeper limitations imposed by the reasoned quality of judgment.

To reveal this limitation, it is useful to situate reason within a historical context. Reason is not something that simply exists and exists as an ideal and perfect way of thinking or making decisions or analysing stuff. It is, rather, a particular method of analysis that emerged through a period known as the European Enlightenment, mentioned in the previous section. The Enlightenment took place across the 16th and 17th centuries (roughly) and was a period characterised by an explosion in artistic and scientific development, which led to modernity.

The Enlightenment involved a shift in terms of the way society was ordered and knowledge of the world was produced. To be modern, after the Enlightenment, is to reject the reliance on natural or divine values or the conventions of tradition and instead to turn to logical thought free from such restrictions. This can be seen in legal thinking (using reasoned logic to ground decisions rather than simply relying on tradition or the divine authority of a sovereign), as well other areas of culture and the arts (think of modernist architecture and design, which is based upon abstract geometric forms rather than ornate or traditionally decorative styles).

Modernity involves using reasoned understanding to ground social structures and decision-making, as well as the production of knowledge. It seeks a perfect or universal understanding of the world and a universally just structure to society and does this by relying on the supposedly 'universal' logic of reason. Recall the Renaissance humanism mentioned in the previous section that relied on such ideals. At the wider level of knowledge and understanding, it is through the Enlightenment that the scientific method developed and the disciplines of the natural sciences emerged, with the rational approach to understanding not only producing new knowledge about the world but seeking a rational order to the organisation of knowledge itself. So the natural sciences were differentiated from the social sciences, as well as from other disciplines such as the arts and humanities. Indeed, this structuring and categorisation of disciplines is an effect of the shift to modernity that sought to order the world according to logic and reason (we discuss this further in Chapter 4). Things needed to be categorised in a logical way, and this resulted in some quite intricate structuring of human knowledge and social life—as well as the detailed doctrines of the modern law.

But with its broad range of interests and effects and its wide social importance, law found itself caught between a range of disciplinary areas. On the one hand, the best way to solve social problems and make 'good' law might be to apply the powerful methods of science, to apply rational, social-scientific approaches to understanding social structure, political power, and the psychology of the population. But the problems of law can also be tackled through more qualitative methods, such as anthropology, which seeks to understand human cultures and values without relying so heavily on scientific methods. Further still, ensuring the best law can also be seen as a concern amenable to understanding through studying the humanities—for example, by analysing how legal meaning is produced (see Chapter 7), or the practice of rhetoric in the form and style of legal presentation (see Chapter 8), or even a critical reflection on the scientific methods that were being used elsewhere.

As a complex question about how to order society—about how to administer a society's reaction to damaging or harmful conduct, about what to do with those who commit crime, about what rules should be in place in an indefinite range of areas of life—law becomes something that can be understood from different disciplines. But it has also retained its links with the legal profession and its traditional context of practical adjudication and legal decision-making, and thus also remains a vocational or technical subject, with its particular methods of case-by-case decision-making (see Chapter 1). This all resulted in the separation of law as a discipline in its own right, and at its extreme, it became limited only to 'doctrinal' methods of close reading, distinguishing cases, treating like cases alike, with reference only to the primary materials of the common law itself (judgments and statutes).

The methods of legal reasoning outlined in the previous section tend towards this doctrinal approach, relying on the form of the decision-making process and its rational procedures to authorise the judgment itself. The legitimacy of the judgment comes not from the knowledge or understanding that is used or the veracity of the information applied by the judges or other external factors but from the mechanisms of reasoning and logic. The idea is that this produces just, general rules that can then be applied again in the future—cases that are 'like' each other would follow the same reasoning and thus produce the same outcome. The resources utilised thus remain those of the common law itself, of previous judgments. This is often called the 'doctrinal' method, or 'black letter' law, because of its sole reliance upon doctrine (traditionally printed in the black letter typefaces of the early printing presses) to the exclusion of other sources. There is, then, quite a clear limitation to this idea of judgment as reasoning, in that important information and understandings about the way law operates in society, about its wider effects and impacts on citizens and members of the population that live under the law, as well as the external questions of authority (see Chapter 2), are quite easily overlooked. There is also an irony in that it seems quite illogical or *unreasonable* to ignore or not use certain areas of knowledge and understanding just because of the discipline or source they might come from.

This extreme doctrinal vision of law still exists today but is tempered by a wider acceptance of a range of methods and approaches to understanding law and the operation of judgment. A new orthodox method of law is known as 'socio-legal studies', which combines rational methods of the social sciences (such as statistics and empirical sociological and psychological studies, as well as sociological theory about social structure and change, and their causes) with doctrinal approaches. The idea is to seek to understand not just what the 'internal' justifications of a particular decision might be, but also to examine the wider effects and impacts of that decision on society and its members in an empirical way (i.e. what actually *is* the nature of society in this context and what is the actual or potential effect of the law).

The question of judgment as reasoning is thus not only concerned with the legal argumentation employed in terms of formal structure and the application of previous case law, but also a wider set of rational examinations and analyses relating to law's social context and influence. But it is variable how often such work consciously influences judicial decision-making—with judges still relying primarily on the processes of reasoning and generalisation characteristic of law and the primary legal materials (cases, statutes) that are seen to be the most authoritative.[5] And again, with the authority of these primary sources stemming from their production by judges through reasoned analysis (see above) while occupying the office of the judge (see Chapter 2).

Underlying all of the discussion so far is a deeper and more profound limitation to reasoned understanding and a limit that permeates pretty much all disciplines. This is the idea that reason itself has certain characteristics and limitations. As we noted above, any method entails limits on what can be understood—and reason is no different. The problem, perhaps, is that because reason is so deeply ingrained in the way we try to understand things—individually and culturally—it becomes difficult to think without it, or to try to conceive of law and legal issues without it, or to make decisions in cases without it. But if we start to describe some of the central defining features of reason, it will hopefully become clear what kind of limits it has, and even some problematic associations it has in terms of equality and justice.

The particular form of modern reason that law relies upon emerged, as we have noted, through the Enlightenment. It is a form of logic and conceptual elaboration that rests upon its divorce from emotional influences. Indeed, one of the leading theories of reasoned understanding comes from Immanuel Kant, who advocated for a strong division between the exercise of reason and emotional or sensory aspects of human experience. Kant's vision is of reason as a universal and objective ideal of conceptual thought that is shared by all 'reasonable creatures'—as humans, we generally have the capacity for reason, and if exercised correctly, this will always result in the same conclusions and understandings.

His basic idea is that we all share reason, and so the way to reason correctly was to do so in a way that what we thought would remain correct for

---

5 For more on this, see Lady Hale, 'Should Judges be Socio-Legal Scholars?' (Socio-Legal Studies Association 2013 Conference Keynote Address, 26 March 2013) <www.supremecourt. uk/docs/speech-130326.pdf>, listed in the 'Further reading' section.

everyone. This amounted to extracting or deriving a principle or rule from our decision and applying it generally to see if it would be harmful or illogical if everyone adhered to the same principle. In this, you might have spotted, is something similar to the methods of legal reasoning outlined above, as well as in Chapter 1: the movement from particular cases or decisions to a generalised rule or principle applicable to all. One of the most overt features of reason, then, is its tendency towards abstraction, to result in general ideas or principles largely divorced from specific contexts or examples of conduct, or from specific cases.

We've already noted how this abstraction might be problematic in terms of overlooking real effects and contexts, an abstraction that socio-legal studies and other interdisciplinary approaches to law seek to rectify. But there are also notable exceptions for Kant in terms of which humans were capable of exercising reason properly—it might be that all 'reasonable creatures' can reason, but for Kant, this does not simply mean everyone. Women, in particular, were rejected from having the capacity for true reasoning, as well as those from various non-European ethnicities; these classes of people did not have the same capacity for reason as white male Europeans. We might try to extract the positive values of reason as a method of resolving disputes in law from Kant's controversial opinions, given the historical age in which he was writing, and simply discard these problematic aspects (of course women and non-Europeans have the capacity for reason). But even if we do this, the shape and quality of reason retain certain connotations and assumptions, even if we try to ignore them—particularly gendered ones but also racial ones.

Reason derives from a white male European perspective on the world, and on social problems and how to resolve them. It prioritises abstract, independent thought, free from the influences of social and political structures or relationships of care. It does not come from the perspectives of women and minorities who have lived potentially very different lives, with different ways of understanding problems and their potential solutions, as well as the nature of communal life. A 'rational' modern law arguably inherits these (largely unacknowledged) assumptions, potentially embedding and maintaining racial and gendered bias within law itself.

In this light, reason can be seen not as the one and only way in which we can understand things, but as a particular historical phenomenon within a range of options of how to undertake legal thinking. And as a form that emerged in a particular historical context, it can be seen to have associations and limitations rather than being simply objective or true. Following this line, we are, in a sense, trying to step outside of reason to see what it is and how it works and whether it is a good method for making judgments that approach justice. The limits of judgment as reasoning are thus not only those in terms of the particular method that is undertaken—the particular form of the reasoning—but also connected with the use of reason itself.

What reason is arguably unable to encounter or meaningfully deal with are important concerns like gender, race, and other questions of difference, as well as emotions and the sensory experience of actual living people. In light of the over-arching goals of law and the legal system—to somehow produce justice or, at the very least, authoritative decisions—limitations in relation to these kinds of wide-ranging issues appear very problematic. A decision is surely not just if it is based solely upon a method that is incapable of really understanding the people in relation to whom the decision is being made.

## 3.3 Irrationality

We have seen that methods of reasoning in legal decision-making can partly authorise judgments but at the same time also produce understandings or give a shape to judgment that is problematically limited. In this section, we interrogate what might be at play in decision-making in terms of things outside of reason and consider the extent to which these 'non-reasonable' aspects might be necessary in terms of producing just decisions or legitimate judgments.

A judgment is a particular expression or written form of the legal decision being made. But the written form does not necessarily contain or fully express everything that a judge or bench of judges might have been feeling or thinking about in relation to the case under decision. The written judgment is the end point of a sequence of discussions, negotiations, and reflections. But if we recall a core aim of a legal or judicial system—to achieve justice—it may be the case that there are concerns of 'justice' that animate and drive the decision being made, with the reasoning or justification working to secure this within the broad structures of precedent and the common law more generally. This can be evidenced by the fact that any particular case may be decided in multiple ways—a phenomenon that can be seen most clearly in the production of dissenting judgments, where one judge disagrees on what the outcome of the case should be. There are also variances between judgments that ostensibly produce the same conclusion, as seen in different judges sometimes presenting their own separate opinions as to why a decision should be made, albeit with the same result as their peers on the bench. The outcome may be the same, but their reasoning is different. But the question here is whether there is something 'beyond' the reasoning being used that plays into the judicial decision.

Some would say not (or, at least, *ideally* not): if you think that law is produced through the formal reasoning that is used, you might say that even if there was something 'beyond' the surface reasoning readable in a judgment, it is irrelevant because we still need the reasoning to justify and enable legitimate judgment. A stronger version of this would say that differences in opinion exist because some judgments are simply more 'correct' than others in that they are reasoned in a better or more appropriate manner. Dworkin, for example, might agree with this—for him there are 'right answers' in legal cases that are achievable through deciding with integrity in relation to the history of previously decided cases.

So, if these procedures of reason can produce different conclusions (rather than always producing a single correct one), this signals at least two possibilities: firstly, that there are limitations or errors involved in the reasoning or its application, or secondly, that there is something shaping or directing the reasoning from outside of reason itself. We discussed elements of the first variety in the preceding two sections, so here we will focus on the second.

Terry Maroney has identified a 'cultural script', an established way of performing judicial duties, that requires judges to deny, reject, or otherwise avoid the influence of emotion in their decision-making. As she outlines it: 'A good judge should feel no emotions; if she does, she should put them aside and insulate the decision making process from their influence.'[6] She calls this the 'persistent cultural script of judicial dispassion', and given the previous two sections, it is easy to see how deep this adherence to the pure methods of rational deduction and logic runs. Indeed, this traditional 'script' that judges should follow is explicitly connected to the Enlightenment values we discussed in the previous section of this chapter:

> It [judicial dispassion] draws much of its power from its deep roots in Enlightenment ideals. Indeed, judicial dispassion has come to be regarded as a core requirement of the rule of law, a key to moving beyond the perceived irrationality and partiality of our collective past.[7]

The main storyline of the Enlightenment tells that the advent and spread of reason steered society away from superstition, unfounded beliefs, and irrational governmental structures. Instead, through the application of reason we can ensure that our public institutions are coherent and defensible—and the decision-making of judges fits into this broader scheme of the modern state. A legal decision is legitimate and has authority only where it is properly rational. Judicial emotions thus exist, in this way of thinking, as a threat to the very order of society and the pursuit of justice. Put in a different light, the rational form of legal judgment is itself necessarily contingent upon irrationality and emotion,

---

6  Terry Moroney, 'The Persistent Cultural Script of Judicial Dispassion' (2011) 99 California Law Review 629, 630.

7  Maroney (n 6) 633.

as the 'other' that it defines itself against. In either version, anything irrational is pushed outside the 'acceptable' form of judgment.

Proper reason might automatically give us justice, but equally it might be that it is a judge's sense of justice or injustice, or other emotional feelings, that give rise to a particular line of reasoning, or that a written and reasoned decision seeks to articulate. We might say that the emotions of a judge can interfere with the 'purity' of their reasoning or judicial conduct, but whether this is a good or bad thing is open for debate—feelings of sympathy and mercy, or the capacity to empathise with those before the court, are arguably central skills required for 'good' judgment, while feelings like hatred or fear might lead to bad or unfair judgments. It is the danger of emotion and irrationality negatively affecting judgment and making them biased or otherwise unfair that underpins the preference for reason and rationality.

Understanding judgment as reasoning to the exclusion of any emotional influence is problematic, primarily in terms of the naïveté in thinking that a judge can both recognise and ignore any emotional influence on their reasoned judgment, but also in terms of robbing judgment of the possibility of employing positive emotional influences such as mercy and empathy (as just noted, emotionality may be a necessary element in rendering a 'good' or just judgment, or justice itself may be something we feel). This problematic exclusion is made worse when we note not only that emotions can operate in both legitimate and illegitimate ways, but that reasoning can also produce injustice if it is incorrect or based on mistaken belief, and other human faculties that judges acceptably employ on a regular basis (e.g. oral communication or memory) can also suffer from their own failures or limitations.

Research into the nature and operation of emotions is quite clear that they are not simply a sea of chaos that exists in opposition to rational certainty. They complement, produce, and direct our rational faculties in various ways—indeed, the ability to reason well may itself be contingent upon emotions.[8] Maroney again:

> If judicial emotion is inevitable, and at least sometimes a positive force, then its value for judging is *normatively variable*. . . . Emotion's normative variability means that it is no more capable of answering hard legal questions than is reason.[9]

---

8 Maroney discusses the research on this point at length, highlighting that emotions not only reveal reason and help us act in accordance with it (because emotions rely upon thoughts and are not just abstract or random feelings) but also enable reasoning itself to unfold, and can be educated or shaped to be more productive and appropriate for judicial use: see Maroney (n 6) 642–651.

9 Maroney (n 6) 671. Emphasis in original.

In making a 'just' decision, then, a judge's feelings of justice or injustice may underpin or give rise to the more concrete reasoning that is actually written into the record of a judgment. But perhaps more significantly than this, or at least going a little further in terms of what this might mean for someone seeking to analyse or otherwise make sense of a judgment that has been made, the presence of emotion or other 'extra-rational' elements within a decision—whether consciously acknowledged in a judgment or a judge's own mind—can open up to an alternative, critical method of 'reading' the common law.

We will return to the potential to read the law in a variety of ways in Chapter 7 (on interpretation), but we should note here the potential to 'get at' the irrational or unconscious elements that may be detectable in the rational written form of judgment. As Peter Goodrich frames it:

> legal rules can never be read literally, nor should their application be understood as purely logical . . . The figures of the legal text indicate those slips or unconscious motives that allow for the reconstruction of 'another scene' of legal judgment . . . The analysis of the figures of the text, of the literary symbols and other values or virtues of justice thus opens up a zone of affectivity [or emotions] . . . The legal text is not immune to a certain politics of judicial affection. The logic of analogy, of things that are both like and liked, is the mechanism which allows the judge to shift from logic to value, from law to justice or from rules to ethics.[10]

In this version, it becomes the desires and preferences of a judge—beyond those that are rationally acknowledged or formally included in a procedure of reasoned logic—that enable a judgment to be made without being a mere mechanical repetition of precedent. As we saw with Goodrich in Chapter 1, bare precedent is akin to anecdote and is thus meaningless as a source of authority without some elaboration, interpretation, and application to the present case. And this meaningful judgment is not just one of reasoned logic but also of feeling and desire. And if we read a judgment with this in mind and pay attention to the little slips and inferences, take them seriously, and examine them in detail, we may be able to identify something of that 'other' impetus for the decision beyond the stated reasons or logical justification.

The ideal of judicial dispassion is a supposed defence against the vagaries of emotion. But what passion and desire actually signal are the capacities

---

10  Peter Goodrich, 'Oedipus Lex: Slips in Interpretation and Law' (1993) 13 Legal Studies 381, 394.

for decision-making to take place. The mere application of a rational process is mechanical and automatic and lacks judgment in any true or meaningful sense. For judgment to take place, the uncertainty and irrationality outside of reason must be acknowledged, opened up, and engaged with, as a process of deliberation and the potential for things to go either way, before a decision is ultimately made.[11] But even if we don't go this far, the point to take is at least to acknowledge the role of the emotional and the irrational within, or as a counter-point to, the procedures of judgment and their complex and debated relationship with the clean, rational form that is supposedly required for legitimate legal decisions.

## 3.4 Further reading

- For a full presentation of MacCormick's theory of judicial reasoning, see Neil MacCormick, *Rhetoric and the Rule of Law: A Theory of Legal Reasoning* (Oxford University Press 2005).
- For discussion of Dworkin's ideas, and specifically how it derives from the traditional methods of Renaissance humanism, see Mark D Walters, 'Legal Humanism and Law-as-Integrity' (2008) 67 Cambridge Law Journal 352. For Dworkin's own rendition, see Ronald Dworkin, *Law's Empire* (Fontana 1986).
- On the emergence of law as distinct amongst the disciplines following the Enlightenment, written by a sitting judge, see Jeanne Gaakeer, *Judging from Experience: Law, Praxis, Humanities* (Edinburgh University Press 2019) 28–45 (chapter 2).
- For reflections on the use of socio-legal methods and insights within judicial decision-making, also written by a sitting judge, see Lady Hale, 'Should Judges be Socio-Legal Scholars?' (Socio-Legal Studies Association 2013 Conference Keynote Address, 26 March 2013) <www.supremecourt.uk/docs/speech-130326.pdf>
- For the racist qualities of law, despite its appearance as a benevolent institution, see Peter Fitzpatrick, 'Racism and the Innocence of Law' (1987) 14 Journal of Law and Society 119. For some recent, brief commentary on this paper, see Patricia Tuitt, 'A Concise Note on Peter Fitzpatrick's "Racism and the Innocence of Law"' (2021) 17 International Journal of Law in Context 36.

---

11 See Jacques Derrida, 'Force of Law: The "Mystical Foundation of Authority"' (1990) 11 Cardozo Law Review 919. A fuller engagement with this idea will be made in Chapters 7 and 9.

- For an advanced introduction to the intricacies of judicial emotions, see Terry Moroney, 'The Persistent Cultural Script of Judicial Dispassion' (2011) 99 California Law Review 629.
- For a fuller discussion on the 'psychoanalytic' method of reading judgments in order to access judicial desire or the unacknowledged influences on decision, see Peter Goodrich, 'Oedipus Lex: Slips in Interpretation and Law' (1993) 13 Legal Studies 381.

# 4 Truth

Combined, the previous chapters present judgment as (ideally) rationally authoritative decision-making. In these ideas, judgment is a process or means of achieving an outcome. In this chapter, however, we shift to exploring judgment as an object of knowledge—something that we can know or that gives us stuff we can know. In approaching judgment this way, we shall consider the relationships between judgment and truth. Truth will be understood in two senses: as something produced by the judicial process (i.e. that judgment authoritatively underwrites the content of judicial statements as 'true' in some way) and as something that is used within judicial decisions (i.e. the 'truth' that judgments use to help make them legitimate).

We shall start by considering the fact/law distinction and the ways factual decisions (i.e. decisions as to what is 'true') can be seen to be a product of the broader features of legal decision-making (section 4.1). We shall then articulate an understanding of judgment as a form of knowledge—with judgments being containers or sources of law themselves rather than simply records of previous decisions (section 4.2). The chapter will finally close with a broader reflection on the disciplinary characteristics of this knowledge, and hence the particular and contingent form of 'truth' that law produces in society (section 4.3).

## 4.1 Fact/law

In legal understanding, fact is often distinguished from law. This is an excellent starting point for thinking about the ways in which judgment can be understood as a form of truth. The fact/law distinction basically consists of the assumption that there are two kinds of things. Firstly, those things that exist as 'facts' out there in the world to be discovered or recorded or explained; things that have happened or that we can simply know. Secondly, those other things, which we call laws or rules, that are not 'things' in the

DOI: 10.4324/9780429329784-4

sense of objects, but are concepts and ideas that we can use to guide decisions based upon facts. This division—between things that happen or exist and the rules that we use govern them—underpins the reasoning processes of law we examined in Chapter 3 and also the idea of judgment as legal decision in Chapter 1. Judgments involve applying law to facts to resolve disputes, treating like cases (that is, similar sets of 'facts') alike.

A distinction between law and fact seems to make a lot of sense, given that things *happen* and then in some situations the law gets involved to decide who wronged whom, to what extent, and how it might be fairly resolved. It also shapes core methods of problem-solving, such as the ILAC method: we first determine what *issue* the facts raise, then what the relevant *law* is, how that law might *apply*, and finally what the legal *conclusion* is. The distinction between fact and law also underpins the supposed three-part structure of judgments. Judgments are commonly understood to be made up of three interconnected elements: 1) facts; 2) the central reasoning behind the decision in the case (sometimes called *ratio decidendi*, translated as 'the reason for the decision'); and, 3) some additional discussion of the law (sometimes called *obiter dicta*, often translated as 'things said by the way'). Like problem-solving methods, this three-part structure of judgment assumes that judgments are legal decisions made about things that happen. The law is discussed, the relevant bits are applied to the facts, and a conclusion is determined. Such is the pragmatic procedure of judgment in court, as much as in academic problem-solving and the drafting of legal advice.

The fact/law distinction may seem to be a somewhat technical one, but it has practical and conceptual implications. It shapes the functioning of court systems, as well as how we think about what law is and how judgments are made. In common law processes, questions of fact and questions of law are answered using different principles and in some cases by different people with different sets of expertise. Indeed, a phenomenon that comes with the fact/law distinction is that the outcome of a case might hang entirely on a factual determination, while another case might have undisputed facts with the outcome then hanging on how the law is understood, interpreted, or applied. Questions of fact in criminal cases, for example, are often determined by laypersons with no legal training (e.g. members of the jury). They decide based upon their own common sense in light of the evidence that has been presented to them at trial. Questions of law, meanwhile, are decided by the judge following argumentation from the parties to the case. In other types of cases, such as civil disputes, the judge may determine fact and law as distinct sets of questions using different sets of rules. Appeals are another example: appeals tend to be permitted for questions of law, with appeals on questions of fact only in exceptional circumstances (e.g. if new evidence comes to light).

Often, cases will be a complex mixture of factual and legal determinations, with some being more contentious or central to the outcome than others. The interplay between law and fact can be tricky to navigate, especially if we recall that judgment is invariably a process of applying general laws to specific facts: it is not only a question of what is a fact, of what actually took place, but also a question of how the law applies to those facts, what legal categories the facts fall into, and how those facts shape the legal determination or outcome. In this complex interplay, the division between facts and laws that apply to them is not as stable as it might first appear. If we are thinking about judgment as truth, the ways in which 'truth' is presented or determined within processes of judgment are worth examining a little further.

Facts are facts, right? They're simply stuff that actually happens or a record of things that have actually happened. We will question this later in this section and across this chapter, but even if we accept this as being the case (facts are simply what happened), the stability of the division between fact and law remains questionable. When we read a judgment, typically the opening sections involve a recounting of the facts of the case—the sequence of events that led to the dispute in issue. These may be quite detailed, with names, relationships, dates, and places all included, amongst other data. But not all of these facts will be important for the legal decision in the case, and there will, of course, be a whole host of facts that are not included in the judicial summary.

For example, the details of who won the Battle of Hastings in 1066 will unlikely be included in most judgments (despite its significance for the history of the common law). Similarly, a case involving murder or theft may include the date(s) upon which events took place or their location(s), but these will likely have no relevance to whether the requirements of those offences have actually been fulfilled by the defendant. In presenting the facts of a case, then, a judgment is already not a simple neutral bystander, transparently recounting what has happened. There are decisions and determinations that are going on, often behind the scenes, in order to piece apart those facts that are completely irrelevant, those that are relevant to the context or background of the case, and those that are more central or upon which the outcome of the whole case might hang.

On top of this, there are rules of evidence that control what is 'let in'. These rules filter empirical events into legally determined facts that can then form the basis of a decision. Some evidence may be inadmissible, even though it did actually happen, and so becomes a 'fact' in a case only in certain circumstances—not simply by virtue of its status as a real event. In this we can see something of a broader feature of case facts, also implied by the previous paragraph: the facts upon which a judgment is based, or that the law is applied to, are not just a record of what happened but are a limited and particular form of description of a sequence of events. They are, for want of a better word, a narrative: they tell a story, with scene setting, characters, motivation, and a beginning, a middle, and an end (for more on judgments as narratives, see Chapter 9).

And this narrative is shaped not only or simply by the things that actually happened (and even if this was the case, a textual description in a judgment cannot fully capture the complexity and reality, or indeed trauma, of the lived events). They are also shaped by what counts as a fact for legal decision-making, what evidence is admissible, and the ways in which judges and judgments are able to encode the preceding events and make them usable for judgment. They are shaped by the reasoning processes of the judge—what is relevant, to what extent—and thus also the tensions at play in terms of the limitations of those processes or their potential influence from irrational factors (see Chapter 3).

For example, in order to make a decision about whether a contract has been breached, the events must be translated from empirical lived reality—from the memories of the parties involved—into words and description that can be recorded in the written form of the judgment, and to which the conceptual structures of contract doctrine (offer, acceptance, performance, etc.) can be applied. The 'facts of the case' are thus produced not through a transparent recording process, whereby events are captured—even in a limited sense—but through a conceptual process and examination underpinned by legal concerns rather than empirical ones. To put in bluntly: law shapes the facts.

What does this mean for the fact/law distinction? We noted above that it is a central division that has practical effects in terms of judicial processes, including who makes which decisions and when a party can appeal. The distinction shapes the understanding and practice of law. But if facts are actually produced through legal processes—that is, they are products of law rather than an objective, unbiased, or transparent record of actual events—does the distinction completely fall down? Is the system built upon an imaginary division that doesn't really exist? And does this matter? These are quite big questions, but one simple way through is to recognise that the fact/law distinction does exist, but it only exists as a legal concept. The distinction between fact and law is not a natural or pre-existing one but one that emerges through the processes and determinations of the common law and its method—that is, through judgment.

The tendency towards generalisation and abstraction that we noted in the preceding chapters—that law is general and applied to specific cases and that this is a product of the doctrine of precedent—shows how this might emerge, with one aspect of each decision breaking away from the specific facts of the individual case and forming or joining with a general rule or principle. That which is specific to an individual case remains as fact, while that which is general becomes doctrine or principle. The fact/law division thereby emerges and is maintained: it does not necessarily precede law or judicial determination or shape it, but is a symptom of the common law method of treating like cases alike.

The thing to remember as we try to understand judgment, as we work with judgments as common law judges, lawyers, scholars, and other students of the law, is that facts are not given but are produced to particular ends via particular methods and thus should attract as much critical analysis and reflection as any other part of a judgment or decision. What this also means is that in thinking about judgments as truth, we are not dealing with a pure, objective truth but a particular production of knowledge as something that goes beyond transparently describing events. We will explain and explore this in more detail in the following section.

## 4.2 Knowledge

We have seen that thinking of judgment as truth has a number of complexities, including the truth of the facts that are employed in judicial decisions and their relationship with the law that is applied to them. This question focuses on the truth of those parts of a judgment that claim to relate to things that have happened 'in real life'. We saw that these real events—when presented in a judgment—lose something of their reality and instead become a product of legal categories and requirements. But there is another side to judgment as truth, which focuses not on the 'factual' aspects of judgment but on the judgment as a whole as a form of truth—or, put differently, as knowledge.

There is something important happening when we speak of knowledge as opposed to truth. Truth has quite overt implications of empirical or factual accuracy, as discussed in the previous section, and knowledge might be said to share some of these associations. We *know* about the world: we know that water boils at 100 degrees Celsius, for example, or that the Earth travels around the Sun. We might know that X stabbed Y with a kitchen knife, and if we apply law to this fact, we might come out with a conclusion of murder or manslaughter. Knowledge and truth have a very complex relationship, but generally a close one—indeed, they might be understood as identical in some circumstances. On one level, knowledge might be 'true' if it fits certain criteria when measured against the real world—X actually did stab Y with a kitchen knife. We might also speak of a subjective notion of truth—if X actually stabbed Y with a fork rather than a knife, then it might still be 'true *for us*' that it was a knife if this is what we 'know' about what happened.

This subjective version of truth is especially relevant when we recognise the limits of our ability to know about things, as indicated in the preceding chapter when we discussed that methods shape or limit understanding. We know about the world only through our senses, albeit sometimes augmented by instruments of measurement such as microscopes or infrared cameras. Our knowledge, then, arguably cannot ever really be compared to the truth of reality because what we can experience of the world is only ever what we can encounter through the methods and perspectives we have available (senses, measurement, experience, etc.). A truth that is absolute or 100% certain is practically impossible, although it might be possible to think that it exists as an ideal or is what we are aiming for. Indeed, the legal system acknowledges this in one of the criminal law's most famous sayings: 'beyond a reasonable doubt'. The truth of the facts held to exist in a criminal case is tested not against whether they are 100% certain, because we can never know that, but instead whether it is reasonable to doubt that they occurred—a much lower standard.

Knowledge, then, is maybe all we have—we can't get to the truth (and this is why there have been thousands of years of philosophical debate over whether there is an absolute truth that we can try to access, with some believing there is, and others believing there is not, and others coming down somewhere else). And knowledge is something that is generated through methods, it is produced by people trying to understand and make sense of stuff—be it boiling water, social inequality, quasars, or what happened when Y died from a stab wound in their kitchen.

But how does this change our understanding of what judgment is? Sure, judgments use knowledge—in the form of facts produced through legal methods—to ground the decision being made. Can we say that judgments are actually, in themselves, knowledge? Or indeed, that they are truth or at least a version or form of truth? The other versions of judgment we have encountered so far would suggest not: judgments are resources to be used to solve problems or disputes; they are an expression of state authority; they are decisions or a certain kind of rational method. These visions of judgment share the characteristic of seeing judgment as more verb than noun: as something that is done rather than as an object to be encountered. We discussed something of this distinction in Chapter 1, with the 'noun' form of judgment (as a resource to be deployed in future cases or legal argumentation) most solidly being understood as shorthand for the 'verb' of the process of judgment: a recorded judgment indicates that, given similar facts (they are like cases), the same outcome would be reached (they would be treated alike). But in thinking about judgment as knowledge, we can understand the ways in which judgments can be objects in themselves rather than as 'shorthand' for a process.

Judgments tell us something. Beyond the outcome or decision of the particular case, they also contain other information or qualities that are of broader relevance: to the parties involved, to the common law, to society and culture. In a judgment is encoded not just a record of a specific judicial decision but also information about a variety of other things. These include, obviously, the legally rendered 'facts' and outcome of the case, but also the examination and discussion of the law that was undertaken, in the form of both the central reason for the decision (*ratio decidendi*) and any broader discussion of doctrine and principle (*obiter dicta*)—itself a distinction that is questionable and often a product of interpretation. More broadly, a judgment can also be a window into a particular set of social or cultural values—indeed, legal historians might think of judgments not as binding authority to be used in legal argumentation but as evidence or resources for understanding what society and legal systems were like in times gone by. Contemporary academics might study judgments as an anthropological, sociological, political, or philosophical resource, examining their various features in an effort to make sense of our current world (culturally, socially, politically, or as a form of moral or ethical thinking).

Judgments thus have various object-like qualities beyond their status as records of the outcome of a decision-making process. These qualities can be thought of as knowledge: by reading a judgment, we come to know about these different aspects. Most centrally, what we come to know about is the law itself: judgments are a huge resource of legal knowledge, of knowledge and understanding and discourse related to the content and features of the law itself. Indeed, this is a central aspect of the common law method: we must compare new cases to the archive of previous cases to see how to treat them. In a practical sense, the idea that judgments are shorthand for how a similar case would be decided becomes the idea that judgments contain general principles of the law itself and, thus, that we can know and understand the law as a conceptual object by reading judgments.

With this, we can see how judgments are more than legal decisions but are a form of legal knowledge (as well as being 'evidence' for other kinds of study, such as history or social studies). They are the truth of law, or they contain a truth that belongs to law—law's truth, if you will. Perhaps most accurately, they are not actually legal truth or knowledge, but instead, they indicate or are the evidence of legal truth or knowledge. Law is actually the conceptual structures of legal doctrine and principle that are produced via the common law method, discussed and examined through judicial processes, and then only captured or recorded in an archive or database from where it can be accessed and studied. In this sense, judgments are the evidence from which knowledge of the law might be derived, not a source of knowledge or truth in themselves—an idea we will return to when we look, for example, at questions of interpretation (Chapter 7) and improvisation (Chapter 9).

## 4.3 Discipline

Understanding judgment as a form of knowledge situates judicial deci-sions within a range of different areas—what we might identify as aca-demic disciplines or areas of scholarly study (that is, areas within which knowledge is produced). Knowledge, like truth and fact, is often thought to be something that we take for granted, that exists, and that we can have in some way—through study or experimentation, for example. But as we have already indicated, things may not be so simple: knowledge is something that is made or developed by those who try to make sense of things. And this knowledge production takes place in different contexts, about different areas of human experience, or through different methods: physics, maths, biology, sociology, history, engineering, linguistics, musicology, botany, lit-erature, philosophy—amongst many others.

These are what we call disciplines, and on one level law is a discipline like any other: it has certain objects and methods of study, things that we try to understand through particular ways of asking and answering questions. While we have seen in previous chapters ways in which law has something that might seem to be different from academic study—in its judicial form as authoritative judgment or reasoned problem-solving that seeks to solve actual disputes and achieve justice, or regulate society through the admin-istration of state power—there is also a disciplinary dimension to judgment as knowledge, as part of the wider academic subject of law or legal studies.

The discipline of law is not quite the same as the profession or system of law, although there is a degree of overlap. For example, understanding judg-ment as truth or knowledge means that what judges do becomes something more than the adjudication of a particular dispute, but can be seen to be a form of scholarship or academic study—but with perhaps wider-ranging and more-concrete impacts than what might be thought of as more tradi-tional academic study (e.g. in universities). Other overlaps include the use of judgments as part of wider academic discourse, or the application of the common law method in academic analysis of real and hypothetical cases. When we think of judgment as part of 'disciplinary' law in this way, what we are thinking of expands quite dramatically from the core decision-mak-ing process of judicial practice that we examined in Chapter 1. Judgment here becomes one (important and interconnected) element within a wider set of materials, sources, and practices that constitute the discipline of law.

In thinking about the disciplinary dimensions of judgment, we are con-sidering ways in which judgment falls into or relates to the academic or scholarly discourses of law more broadly understood. What we are also thinking about is the impact or effects of this disciplinary form of law, this particular kind of knowledge production. Its effects in terms of how disputes might be resolved, of how individuals or their experiences might be understood or represented in legal knowledge (in judgments), and, more generally, the impact of the form or structure of legal knowledge on how justice might be achieved and societies might be governed.

These questions arise most profoundly when it is remembered that judgment, and law more generally, is connected with power and authority. There is a powerful aspect to legal judgment (see Chapter 2) that is part of its practical, adjudicative function, as well as underpinning the desire to ensure it is done as justly as possible. As they say, power and responsibility come in equal measure. In order to properly understand the impacts and effects of judgment as a form knowledge, we need to understand the relationships between law as a powerful force and as a discipline. As we will see, the basic relationship here is one of integration—disciplinary knowledge and power can be seen to be deeply interlinked, not just in law but across society.

In order to elaborate this idea of the interconnection of power and knowledge, we will turn to the philosophy of Michel Foucault, who spent his career trying to make sense of how power operates in modern society and the ways in which institutions and knowledge-making enable or articulate the operation of power. Like judgment, discipline has both a noun and a verb form. And Foucault's ideas are about discipline in both of these senses: as an area of academic knowledge or study (*a* discipline) and as a normalising force or power (*to* discipline).

How does power operate? One instinctive idea, and perhaps a familiar one for those who have read Chapter 2, is that power is held or wielded by a particular person or office, and that it is structured in a hierarchy. The head of a company is in charge, with deputies or senior managers following them, with middle managers beneath them, all the way down to the workers on the shop or factory floor. A president or monarch of a country is in charge of that country, with cabinet ministers or knights of the realm following them, followed by other public officials. What Foucault was interested in, however, was how this kind of hierarchical or top-down form of power might be changing in modern societies. This is important for understanding judgment as truth, as it goes to the question of the power of judgment and the judicial system to produce or authorise 'legal truth'—that is, the official knowledge and understanding of the law that we have just outlined.

What Foucault basically observed was a shift from top-down power to a more fluid and complex network of relations, with power being not simply something we can hold or use within hierarchical organisations but something that flows throughout society and is at work in nearly all relations between individuals—but especially where those relations are institutional. Two of the most famous examples Foucault used can be found at the opening of his book *Discipline and Punish*.[1] While often cited, the two examples that form his introduction to this book demonstrate much of what he is examining across his philosophical career.

The first example he recounts is that of a man called Damiens, who is brutally and publicly tortured and executed for regicide. The second example is a list of mundane activities that recounts the routine of the inhabitants of a prison. There is less than a century separating these two examples, and Foucault essentially asks what has happened between them: both are punishment, but one is an overtly violent public spectacle, while the other is a hidden and relatively boring daily routine. Foucault traces a broad shift between two models of power: the execution of Damiens represents a top-down and highly public display of power, while the prison routine represents a more subtle, complex, net-like power that permeates society in a more covert way. It is this second form of power that is linked with modern disciplinary knowledge, notably in the way it raises questions of how power can be exercised through the production of knowledge about individuals.

While our concern here is with judgment, a key insight of Foucault's ideas is that this exercise of power exceeds the boundaries of the state, with power operating in a wide variety of contexts (Foucault studied, amongst other things, the medical profession, psychiatry, criminal justice, and religion). The modern, net-like power that Foucault identifies is something that can be seen across society. While the old top-down power operated through the hierarchical exercise of force and, in many ways, needed to be seen to be maintained (hence the public nature of punishment in the example of Damiens), the modern net-like power operates much more subtly and on a much smaller or more intimate scale.

This is important for thinking about judgment, because the typical vision of judgment is of a powerful judge (with some kind of authority, whatever it might be or wherever it might come from—see Chapters 2 and 3) handing down a decision that not only binds the parties to the case but also future parties in similar circumstances. This is a top-down vision of power, with the judgment—the law—existing at the pinnacle of the hierarchy, controlling or determining the fate of those under its influence. The law, courts, and judges hold or wield power and exercise it through the making of judgments. With the suggestion that judgments are not simply a reasoned

---

1 Michel Foucault, *Discipline and Punish: The Birth of the Prison* (Alan Sheridan tr, Penguin 1977).

exercise of authority that makes a legal decision but are also a form of knowledge in themselves, we thus open up to the disciplinary or net-like power of judgment. And in this we see not only that judgments are part of the wider discipline of law, but are part of a general circulation of Foucault's 'disciplinary power' throughout modern society.

This net-like disciplinary power is characterised by normalisation. This means it does not see power as something objectively existing but as shaped by ideas of normativity that are contingent on different contexts and kinds of understanding. Education is a good example: there is not some 'right' way of knowing or understanding the world, there is not some 'true' form of knowledge or method, but rather there are common or 'normal' ways of doing things within particular academic subjects or disciplinary areas. Through an educational journey, by being taught and assessed, individuals are measured and ranked against these norms through the allocation of grades: that is, judgments are passed over individuals in terms of how they relate to these norms.

Medicine is another good example: there is not some objectively 'correct' way in which bodies should function, but there is a supposed 'normal' or 'ideally functioning' body established as medical knowledge, against which individual bodies are measured, with medicine operating to 'normalise' them towards the idealised norm. Morality and crime, too: there are not objective standards of right and wrong, but rather supposed norms against which individuals are judged, with the penal system then seeking to normalise or 'correct' individuals towards the 'proper' standards of conduct.

Another example: psychiatry. Psychiatrists study and examine individuals in terms of how their minds work and the mind's relationship with the physical body and develop a body of knowledge about the embodied human mind. This knowledge involves understanding how the mind 'normally' operates in general. Specific individuals are then examined or assessed, and placed in relation to these norms, and—if deemed necessary—are treated in an effort to 'correct' them, to get them back to 'normal'.

In all of these examples and others (the regulation of productivity in factories, for example), there is an examination of individuals, the determining of a 'norm' based on this examination, and a determination as to how the specific individual relates to or deviates from this supposed norm. That is, knowledge is produced about the individual, including knowledge of their deviation from a supposed norm. Through all of this, the exercise of reason is deeply embedded. As we saw in Chapter 3, during the Enlightenment, the widespread application of reason led to the development not only of increased knowledge about the world but also increased structuring and division of that knowledge and the emergence of academic disciplines.

These disciplines were largely the product of reason, and this process can be seen in Foucault's ideas too: working on the 'modern' assumption that reason is a really good way to understand the world by ordering and making sense of it through logic, in Foucault's understanding of discipline it is the application of reason that tends to shape the exercise of power. Psychiatry again: before the Enlightenment, madness and insanity were associated with unknowable, sometimes divine, forces—potentially either good or evil. Through the evolution of psychiatry, reason was applied to understanding madness, and it was redefined as a deviation from a particular idea of normal, rational mental operation. What was previously part of a wide variety of human experiences—linking the mysteries of the human condition with the mysteries of the universe—became medicalised and separated out from what it meant to be a 'proper' or normal human being.[2]

Overall, Foucault claims that this broad shift is characteristic of modern power, which moves from power as something hierarchical (potentially stemming from a divine source: see Chapter 2) to power as something that is exercised through reasoned logic and rational knowledge production—and thus, also, something that is exercised far beyond the hierarchies of the state.[3]

We can trace the development of law and legal thinking within this broad change. The most obvious shifts come in the form of the rise of reason and rationality as a core method in legal understanding and practice. Premodern law (e.g. during the medieval period) lacked the degree of structure and formality that we see today. It operated predominantly through hierarchical relations based on land ownership and personal relationships with the monarch. This led to wide variation in how law was exercised and how justice was achieved (and what it meant) from town to town, case to case. The core method of the common law—treat like cases alike—had not yet taken hold; it was not always a professional judiciary that exercised judgment, and decisions were not systematically reported. These systems only developed later, as the state became larger and more rationally organised following the Enlightenment.

And this is precisely the point we can draw from Foucault in our analysis of judgment: law moved from being an exercise of power that was held or wielded by particular people or offices (and not always consistently and not always logically or fairly) to being a wide-scale rationalisation of social life

---

2  See Michel Foucault, *History of Madness* (Jonathan Murphy and Jean Khalfa trs, Routledge 2006).

3  For discussion on the escape of power from the state, see James Martel, 'Why Does the State Keep Coming Back? Neoliberalism, the State and the Archeon' (2018) 29 Law and Critique 359, listed as 'Further reading' in Chapter 2.

based upon general norms, with common law judgments operating to determine what those norms were as general principles, how specific parties sat in relation to them, and what might need to be done to correct or rectify that relation. With this, we return to the practical side of judgment. Recognising the disciplinary character of judgment as the practical exercise of coercion or normalisation, it becomes something that is indistinct from the production of knowledge and can be seen as a central feature of modern knowledge itself. Discipline as both noun and verb.

Understanding judgment as truth means recognising it not as something that is distinct from facts but as something that produces those facts for its own purposes or under its own requirements. It means recognising that it is a form of knowledge, a production of a legal truth or the truth of law. And moreover, this exposes the ways in which law is linked into the broader cultural and ideological shifts that took place across the Enlightenment in terms of the modern rational organisation of knowledge and its role in the dissemination and exercise of power throughout society. This brings us full circle back to the authoritative nature of judgment examined in Chapter 2 but also indicates that this is not something distinct or exclusive to the office of the judge: power is exercised in this way across society—in hospitals, schools, workplaces, universities, prisons—in the microscopic or intimate relations between members of society that give rise to knowledge.

## 4.4 Further reading

- For discussion on the rationalisation of law as an academic discipline, with a particular focus on the development of legal education and the form of 'the textbook', see David Sugarman, '"A Hatred of Disorder": Legal Science, Liberalism and Imperialism' in Peter Fitzpatrick (ed), *Dangerous Supplements: Resistance and Renewal in Jurisprudence* (Duke University Press 1991).

- For an example of Foucault's work on the nature of power and its relationship with individuals, see Michel Foucault, 'The Subject and Power' (1982) 8 Critical Inquiry 777. For a fuller example of his work, focusing on law and discipline, see Michel Foucault, *Discipline and Punish: The Birth of the Prison* (Alan Sheridan tr, Penguin 1977).

- Nietzsche's classic essay 'On Truth and Lies in a Non-Moral Sense' is a good introduction to the constructed and perspectival nature of human knowledge and can be found in various versions and translations. We also discuss it directly in the next chapter.

- On the way our own perspective is often hidden within Western legal knowledge and the critical mode of revealing the implications of this, see Desmond Manderson, 'Bodies in the Water: On Reading Images More Sensibly' (2015) 27 Law and Literature 279.

- For a more advanced discussion of perspectival knowledge in a legal context, explored as part of a much larger engagement with the spatial expanse that law (and humans) 'rupture' into knowable chunks (i.e. we cannot 'see' the world from outside since we are inside it), see Chapter 2 of Andreas Philippopoulos-Mihalopoulos, *Spatial Justice: Body, Lawscape, Atmosphere* (Routledge 2015) (and that work more generally).

# 5 Technology

Following from the previous chapter, in which we started to think about judgments as an object of knowledge rather than a process of dispute resolution, the current chapter considers judgment as technology. Judgment as technology is perhaps not the most obvious sense in which we might understand either judgment or technology. But judgment is taken in this chapter again as an object but one that is used to do something—and thus, in this sense, as a technology. But what is it a technology *for*? And how does it work?

We will begin with the most obvious function, beyond the specific resolution of disputes, which is the governance of society (section 5.1). Beyond its purpose, judgment as technology also needs to work—so we will turn next to consider a central technology that judgment relies upon in order to function, namely language (section 5.2). If judgment is technological, and is perhaps also rational or logical (see Chapter 3), then perhaps it can be programmed in advance or automated. The chapter thus closes by considering some contemporary interactions with emerging technologies, specifically in relation to the potential for emulating or replacing human judgment with automated versions using technologies such as artificial intelligence (section 5.3).

## 5.1 Governance

When we consider the role that judicial pronouncements have in affecting how society is organised and how individuals can conduct their lives and relate to each other, it is possible to understand judgments as a technology. Broadly understood, technology is not only electronic or digital devices but can be framed as a larger set of tools or systems that humans use to augment or change their capacity to do things. Phones let us talk over vast differences; doors let us walk through walls; writing lets us record information

DOI: 10.4324/9780429329784-5

outside our bodies; vehicles let us travel faster and further. In a legal context, judgment is a sophisticated tool for doing something in society, namely helping to regulate or govern disputes and other lawful relations. In this sense, it is a technology of governance.

Indeed, judgments are part of a broader apparatus of the state that governs society. Integrated into other parts of the state system (prisons, police, military, various other arms of the civil service, highway maintenance, market regulators, and so on), the courts govern society—however effectually. Adopting this perspective, we are straight away back in the territory of Chapter 2 and questions of the legitimacy of these governmental activities, but we are also still within the realm of Chapter 4: judgment as truth or knowledge that governs through normalising power or discipline. Indeed, in many ways the concern with governance in this section follows directly from the discussion of discipline at the end of the previous chapter.

The current section briefly looks at ideas of biopolitics, which is an area of concern that comes out of the work of Foucault, as well as more recent developments, notably by people like Giorgio Agamben. A lot of stuff has been written related to biopolitics, but we shall focus on outlining the most relevant features for our understanding of judgment as technology: notably, the question of the 'apparatus' of governance. Agamben, in his imaginatively titled essay 'What is an Apparatus?', considers some of the kinds of things that might be considered an apparatus and how we might understand it as a technology of governance. Agamben's conception is very broad:

> I shall call an apparatus literally anything that has in some way the capacity to capture, orient, determine, intercept, model, control, or secure the gestures, behaviors, opinions, or discourses of living beings. Not only, therefore, prisons, mad houses, the panopticon, schools, confession, factories, disciplines, juridical measures and so forth [these are all examples Foucault studies] . . . but also the pen, writing, literature, philosophy, agriculture, cigarettes, navigation, computers, cellular telephones and—why not—language itself, which is perhaps the most ancient of apparatuses.[1]

Technology is thus understood here as anything that seeks or has the effect of controlling or (in Foucaultian terms) normalising individuals. A term that Foucault invented to describe this is subjectivation: subjecting individuals to a technology or form of knowledge, turning them into a 'subject' of that

---

1 Giorgio Agamben, 'What Is an Apparatus?' in *What is an Apparatus? And Other Essays* (David Kishik and Stefan Pedatella trs, Stanford University Press 2009) 14.

knowledge. What does that mean? It's an odd way of looking at things, but it recognises that there is a distinction between living individuals and the knowledge we can have of them—an issue we discussed in more general terms in the previous chapter, where knowledge was understood to be limited by the methods or perspectives we have. Knowledge is not necessarily the same as the thing we are trying to understand. It is also linked up with the exercise of power (a power that circulates in society, articulated by and within relations between individuals in contexts of knowledge production; see Chapter 4). Putting these things together, we get the idea of subjectivation: individuals are subjected to the scrutiny of those who produce knowledge; they are or they become 'subjects' in the collision of 'apparatus' and 'individual'. We thus have a medical subject understood within the discipline of medicine, we have a criminal or penal subject understood within the criminal justice system, and we have a legal subject as the individual understood or articulated within the discourse and knowledge of law (which, of course, includes judgments).

And this is one of the central questions of biopolitics: the way living beings become politicised (biopolitics: the politics of life). This is a central concern for law and judgment, given that the practice of the common law, and the state institution of law more generally, is largely about the relationships between individuals and the state—about how the state deals with or treats the individuals who are party to any specific case, how it does so in a way that achieves or approaches justice, and thus, more widely, how the state treats or manages its citizens, or subjects, in general. In Agamben's version of the apparatus, we find a description of this relationship. Agamben has read lots of Foucault and follows some of the same ideas around power and knowledge; accordingly, an 'apparatus' is a technology of 'knowing' as well as a technology of power. It is something that enables individuals to be governed—to be politicised or to be a political subject of a state or sovereign power.

This is the sense in which it is a technology—it is something beyond the individuals using it that allows them to do something they would not be able to do otherwise, or not be able to do as efficiently, quickly, or successfully. In this case: governing or managing the population of an entire country. Framing judgment as an apparatus, it is something that enables individuals to be governed by law—to be captured and understood and managed by legal ideas, doctrines, and principles, and legal knowledge more generally. It may not be the only one, but judgment is a 'machine of governance'[2]—and an important one, given its position as arbiter of last resort (see Chapter 1).

---

2 Agamben (n 1) 20.

The critical question for we students of the law, of course, is whether this is just. Whether the subjectivation of individuals to the law through judicial opinion enables or produces justice. There are multiple senses or levels to this question—as many, in fact, as there are opinions about what justice itself might be. Examples in relation to the idea of judgment as a technology of governance or apparatus include the following: the way the individual is described or captured in the statements or language of law, the way the apparatus is used or the effects it has in society, the ethics of placing individuals under technologies of power in this way, the legitimacy of that power or the authority of the apparatus (see Chapter 2 again)—and this is even before we get to substantive questions over whether a particular rule might itself be right, wrong, or something else.

Indeed, these questions are big ones in relation to the institution of law. Justice is not just about the substance of rules and about the values we want to hold people and society to, but also about the way those values are administered or instituted and the bureaucratic form that they take. In this sense, judgment as technology becomes particularly important because it recognises that there is something about judgment—about its correctness, justness, or otherwise—that does not relate to its content but simply to the way it operates. And this is not just in the sense of using particular methods of reasoning, as explored in Chapter 3, but is in terms of the material form of judgment and the technologies that it uses, as we explore in the next section.

## 5.2 Language

When initially thinking about the uses of technology in the administration of justice, it is likely that images of satellite surveillance, integrated computer systems, and high-tech security controls might come to mind. Hopefully, the previous section has served to dispel much of this and to enable a broader conception of what the technologies involved in the administration of justice might entail. We will encounter something of the more 'digital' contexts of technology in the final section of this chapter when we look at the implications for judgment of using algorithms or artificial intelligence to try and automate judicial outcomes. In the current section, however, we are concerned with a more mundane technology of justice but also one that is thereby arguably more important or central in terms of the exercise of judgment. The technology we are talking about is language. And we will be thinking not just about language itself but the technologies of written communication that enable its articulation and dissemination.

To a large extent, modern systems of judgment are contingent upon linguistic communication and technologies of writing. The practical dimensions of the judicial system involve activities such as oral debate and hearing, argumentation, discussion, reading, researching, deliberation, interpretation, writing, and dissemination. Judges hear a case, with each side presenting their arguments variously in written and spoken form, and then make their decision as to the outcome, either speaking or writing down the reasons for that decision, with written court records and transcripts being kept and important cases being reported (edited, reproduced, and disseminated) more widely (as noted in Chapter 1). Spoken and written language permeates all of these activities.

Arguably, without such capacities for language, legal and judicial systems such as the Western common law would not be able to exist. There are many senses in which law is something distinct from or more than language—at least in the sense of alphabets and words and speech—such as the performance or ritual of the trial or the architecture of courtrooms (see Chapter 6), or the conceptual ideas of doctrine or the sense of justice (see Chapter 3). It might be controversial to say, then, that law *is* language or that law *is* text, or written words. Instead, the observation we are making here is that in a deeply practical and material sense, modern legal systems require language in order to run—it is part of their hardware, if you will. And more specifically, that the technologies of language and writing are important in understanding judgment within such systems.

The technology of judgment is enabled or underpinned by the technologies of language. This central place of language within practices of judgment has a number of effects. We discussed the impact of method in Chapter 3, and here it raises its head again: technological methods (as much as conceptual ones) shape and limit what it is possible for a system to do. Here, discussing judgment as technology—and specifically as a linguistic technology—the limiting factors of this technological 'choice' become important. A simple example can help indicate part of what these limits involve.

If you can, go outside and pick a leaf. Or if you prefer, imagine a real leaf—perhaps one you have encountered yourself. Compare, if you will, that 'real' leaf with the word *leaf* written in this book. You will hopefully notice that there are quite radical material differences between the printed *leaf* and the 'real' leaf. You could also compare it to a photograph of a leaf or an artist's sketch. Again, other differences will become apparent. The choice of representative technology (word, photo, sketch) changes what is perceived in more or less subtle ways—but all of these representations are quite different from the 'real' leaf. This representational deficiency or deviation is one of the key limitations of the technology of language: no matter how vivid a description, how detailed and seemingly precise, it will never be the same as the 'real' thing and will never fully reproduce a lived object or event.

Timothy Morton gives a nicely poetic phrase that articulates something of this: 'The more I try to show you what lies beyond this page, the more of a page I have.'³ The more detail and information we give about the 'real' world when we're trying to describe or reproduce it in textual form, the more text we need to use—and never do we get to the 'real thing' while we are looking at text. Philosopher Friedrich Nietzsche explains something of this deficiency, too, connecting it to the conceptualisation of generic objects (a leaf) that never exists in reality the way that actual leaves do:

> Every concept arises from the equation of unequal things. Just as it is certain that one leaf is never totally the same as another, so it is certain that the concept 'leaf' is formed by arbitrarily discarding these individual differences and by forgetting the distinguishing aspects. This awakens the idea that, in addition to the leaves, there exists in nature the 'leaf': the original model according to which all leaves were perhaps woven, sketched, measured, colored, curled, and painted—but by incompetent hands, so that no specimen has turned out to be a correct, trustworthy, and faithful likeness of the original model . . . What then is truth? A movable host of metaphors, metonymies, and anthropomorphisms . . . to be truthful means to employ the usual metaphors . . . [it] is the duty to lie according to fixed convention, to lie with the herd and in a manner binding upon everyone.⁴

We can see echoes here of the way the common law method produces general principles by transcending or 'forgetting' the specifics of the individual cases from which they derive (more likely, the common law is symptomatic of the process of abstraction that Nietzsche is describing). And for judgment—which relies as a central technology upon textual description and articulation—this limitation can be quite profound.

If we think about some important things that judges may need to understand and describe while making and communicating their judgments, we might well list objects, like leaves, trees, fields, cars, roads, houses, kitchen knives, and so on. But also, things like agreements, relationships, corporations, property—and, relating to all of this, people. If we are trying to make a just decision, there is a strong sense in which we should be able to properly speak of the things we are making decisions about. Yet conceptualisation and its description or linguistic articulation are limited in relation

---

3  Timothy Morton, *Ecology Without Nature: Rethinking Environmental Aesthetics* (Harvard University Press 2007) 30.

4  Friedrich Nietzsche, 'On Truth and Lies in a Non-Moral Sense' in Patricia Bizzell and Bruce Herzog (eds), *The Rhetorical Tradition: Readings from Classical Times to the Present* (Bedford 1990) 891.

to real, living people. Interestingly, they are also limited with respect to purely conceptual ideas that they might seek to describe (such as companies, agreements, principles, and so on). And this augments the limitations of reason in Chapter 3, where things beyond rational logic were seen to also shape judicial decisions. Similarly, with language, there are significant aspects of judgment that are outside of the textual record, outside of the 'judgment' as an object we can download, read, and apply. (Note, also, how these issues move along similar lines to the questions of truth from Chapter 4, with knowledge always being limited by our experience.)

A second effect of the linguistic technology of judgment is connected to the institutional context of judgment as part of a wider state system. If judgment is based upon the inscription of language, we can observe that this technology (or material method) is integrated into a wider system of material inscription, a wider set of practices that also rely on writing and documents in order to administer justice. This wider system can be understood as bureaucracy. And this system is what connects the written form of law and judgment, and the central place of technologies of writing in the running of legal systems, with the question of authority or sovereign power that we discussed in Chapter 2.

Bureaucracy, in this sense, is a set of practices and hierarchical organisations that revolve around or are underpinned by the use of written documents and files. While we can describe the state in many ways around the idea of authority, power, and sovereignty, in a more material sense, what makes up the state or enables its operation is not some awesome or divine force, but paperwork. Filing the correct form to the correct person has concrete effects—things happen. Writing a judgment and submitting it to record has effects—someone loses their liberty, or someone is awarded damages. And this, of course, reveals that power is still there, that force is still at work, even in the most mundane system of bureaucratic administration. Occupying the office of judge enables access to the paperwork, and the routes via which to submit it, to have such powerful or forceful outcomes. Bureaucratic systems and technologies spread power out; they enable its widespread articulation and navigation by individuals who would not otherwise be able to produce such effects. And underpinning these administrative systems is communications technology—writing.

A third effect connects back to the question of reason, specifically the linguistic logic of argumentation. Arguments and analysis—the reasons for decisions—are captured and communicated through written judgments and must therefore explain those decisions satisfactorily in that written form. In other words, written judgments should be persuasive or convincing to those who read them. In a system of treating like cases alike, they arguably should also give some general reasons or doctrines that can be reused in future similar cases. It is not enough that judges might follow the 'correct' reason, as discussed in Chapter 3—they must also capture this reason in writing. Accordingly, we end up with doctrines and principles that take the form of particular codified statements: written language formulated in a particular way. This might be in the shape of a multi-part 'test' (such as the two-part test for indirect intention in *mens rea* in English criminal law) or as a general statement of principle (such as the principle that a 'free, voluntary and informed' act will break the chain of causation). In either case, it is the turn of phrase that is recorded and survives to be redeployed in the future. In this, we see the interlinking of the material technologies of language and writing with the more conceptual tools of logical reasoning, giving rise to the rational texts of law. (We will explore some of these aspects in more detail when we consider interpretation and rhetoric in Chapters 7 and 8, respectively.)

## 5.3 Automation

If judgment is a technology—a means of governance built upon the rational articulation of logic through language; one technology built upon another—then this raises an interesting and potentially disturbing question. Given recent advances in computing and the development of algorithms capable of making rudimentary analytical decisions, can we programme more advanced technologies to fulfil the same functions as judgment? And what might this tell us about judgment itself? For example, can we create an algorithm capable of reading, digesting, and applying the various and complex protocols and rules of law? If law is built upon rational logic, the idea goes, surely a computer can be programmed to follow that same logic? With this suggestion, we are moving again to a different framing of the question of judgment and technology. Is judgment a form of technology that can be programmed with certain protocols and outcomes, or—if it is to be just—is it a system that necessarily requires 'human' input and guidance? Could we have an AI or robot judge, and could they make just decisions?

To consider this question and its implications, we need to consider the range of functions or 'operations' that are involved in judgment as a mode of legal decision-making, and consider how an automated digital version of those processes might operate or be imagined, and what impact such systems might have on the interests of justice. It is important to note first that reason and logic, as we explored in Chapter 3, are not unproblematic or perfect methods for administering justice through judicial decision-making. Even if it were the case that we could codify the common law into a set of logical protocols and programme them into a computer environment capable of parsing them all in relation to specific cases or sets of facts, this would still be hampered by the same limitations as a purely rational logic of judgment. But with the added problem that these limitations would likely not be mitigated by the influence of discretion or other helpfully 'human' dimensions of judgment.

Indeed, in the context of AI, there is a range of factors that go into the making of judgments that may not be accounted for properly or that may not be included because they are not part of the 'logic' of rational decision-making. As we noted in Chapter 3, it might be that irrational or unacknowledged elements are required if we are able to sense (in)justice in the various guises it might take—and this factor may make fully 'AI judges' improbable (if not impossible). But it also means that if an AI judge's operation is based upon a model of judgment as a form of reasoning, whose processes we can identify and programme into a computer system, then not only are various influential factors in judgment not accounted for, but other factors may also be 'built into' the system in a way that is harmful or inappropriate. For example, a logic-based system of judgment may not be able to fully take into account (either to include or exclude) immaterial things, like value, feeling, culture, meaning, and so on, or the complexities of social context and lived experience.[5]

In a different way, the programming of an AI judge would need to be done by people with the required computational and technological expertise—not necessarily the correct expertise required to be a good judge or to hold the office of judge. The inputting of a legal code into a programmed system or the training of an algorithm by those without judicial proficiency runs a very real risk of embedding into such judicial systems factors and processes that lack appropriate insight and public oversight. The lack of transparency of automated decisions would also permeate the decisions themselves, which would not be available to the same degree of human scrutiny, being made within the complex depths of a computer system rather than openly in reasoned discourse in court and recorded in written documents that can be analysed. Judgment would become, at least in part, a private enterprise, formed and operated beyond the purview of any publicly accountable office.[6]

One of the main methods of training new AI systems to operate is to train them on a large diet of previous examples so that the algorithm gets used

---

5  For discussion of this point, see Tania Sourdin, 'Judge v. Robot: Artificial Intelligence and Judicial Decision-Making' (2018) 41 UNSW Law Journal 1114.

6  Further discussion on the lack of public oversight of AI systems can be found in Francesco Contini, 'Artificial Intelligence and the Transformation of Humans: Law and Technology Interactions in Judicial Proceedings' (2020) 2 Law, Technology and Humans 4.

to producing the right kind of output given certain kinds of input. These models of machine learning, which train algorithms on existing datasets and outcomes, mean that new systems of judgment are simply taught to mimic or replicate old outcomes. This would arguably result in judgment algorithms that are limited in their ability to cope with unexpected or novel cases that are not anticipated by the rules already laid down. And this would have the effect of re-embedding systemic injustices, such as the racial or gender bias of reason or the assumptions of patriarchy noted in Chapter 3. It would also remove the potential for dealing with novelty or unexpected situations or for producing reform.

The wider legal, social, and cultural benefits of the production of written judicial reasoning would be also lost. The function of judgment, as previous chapters have already begun to elaborate, is not simply resolving individual disputes or conflicts. As Sourdin notes:

> Judicial commentary informs how society can operate and many judges also play a role in an educative sense, both informing litigants and lawyers about approaches to be taken and also contributing to civic education at a broader level.[7]

Indeed, as we have already seen ourselves, there are important moral and social values in the dissemination of judgments—not just in terms of the outcomes granted but in terms of the reasoning and analysis that they entail and their status as an object of knowledge (see Chapter 4).

Nevertheless, there are some functions that are perhaps more amenable to automation, such as trawling through large databases to find relevant materials and case reports. But there is a difference between discovering relevant documents and analysing them in light of the applicable law. It is this second process involved in judgment—reasoning and analysis—that is the more complex one to consider in the context of AI and automation. A computer system may be able to work within a system made up of distinct elements and their logical relationships, but that is not the same as understanding what these things mean or their impact in a society populated with humans or navigating the potentially infinite complexities of communal life. Indeed, Morison and Harkens note the importance of judgments by professional judges in navigating this complexity:

> The potential . . . for almost limitless indeterminacy, where novel arguments could be deployed almost indefinitely, is controlled by the wider

context of legal practice in a social process, mediated by judges and conditioned by a whole range of broader professional, social and economic factors within the overall legal system.[8]

And for an AI to do the same is a big ask, involving not only big data analytics but also the interpersonal management of the parties involved in a case. The potential for the reduction of judicial innovation and reform (arguably a necessity for genuinely just decisions: see Chapter 9), or the potential to exercise discretion or to resist rules in cases where their bare 'logic' might produce injustice, are additional concerns with such AI systems.

This is not to say that an AI judge is necessarily impossible. But adding all these issues together, the creation of a satisfactory AI judge has some significant hurdles to jump. This is, in large part, due to the complexity and inherent uncertainty that characterises the law in general and judgment in particular. And this is perhaps the key lesson to draw from this example of judgment's interaction with technology with respect to understanding judgment itself. It is often assumed that law is certain, that it is there to be learned and understood—that cases have right answers. But if we take automation as an exercise or thought experiment and in line with other discussions in this book, it is evident that achieving predictable outcomes to legal questions—as if law is a rational and knowable system—is extremely difficult, if not impossible.

## 5.4 Further reading

- On the idea of the 'apparatus' or the technological for of governance, see Giorgio Agamben, 'What Is an Apparatus?' in *What is an Apparatus? and Other Essays* (David Kishik and Stefan Pedatella trs, Stanford University Press 2009).
- For a detailed analysis of law's reliance upon 'cultural technologies' that enable material articulation, see Cornelia Vismann, 'Cultural Techniques and Sovereignty' (2013) 30 Theory, Culture and Society 83. Fuller elaboration of Vismann's ideas, through analysis of the history of the modern state as the development of filing technologies, can be found in Cornelia Vismann, *Files: Law and Media Technology* (Geoffrey Winthrop-Young tr, Stanford University Press 2000).
- On the limitations of linguistic knowledge—amongst other things—see Friedrich Nietzsche, 'On Truth and Lies in a Non-Moral Sense'.

---

8 John Morison and Adam Harkens, 'Re-engineering Justice? Robot Judges, Computerised Courts and (Semi) Automated Legal Decision-making' (2019) 39 Legal Studies 618, 630.

The version cited in this book is found in P Bizzell and B Herzberg (eds), *The Rhetorical Tradition: Readings from Classical Times to the Present* (Bedford Books 1990), but versions are available in many different volumes, translations, and editions. The title is also sometimes translated differently as 'Truth and Lies in an Extra-Moral Sense'.

- On the (limited?) potential for artificially intelligent systems to automate or replicate processes of legal judgment, see John Morison and Adam Harkens, 'Re-engineering Justice? Robot Judges, Computerised Courts and (Semi) Automated Legal Decision-making' (2019) 39 Legal Studies 618. A useful alternative discussion of the uses of automated technologies in judicial settings can be found in Tania Sourdin, 'Judge v. Robot: Artificial Intelligence and Judicial Decision-Making' (2018) 41 UNSW Law Journal 1114.

# 6 Performance

A judgment is a performance. From the chapters so far, we might broadly say that judgment is made up of decisions that resolve social, moral, and interpersonal conflicts (Chapter 1) through their authoritative (Chapter 2) use of reason (Chapter 3), which also give rise to a kind of judicial knowledge (Chapter 4) that tends to be articulated through writing and becomes a technology of governance (Chapter 5). In each of these chapters, we have also examined some limits and possible alternatives to these aspects of judgment. In the current chapter, we recall that judgment is not only something produced (a noun), but also something that is done (a verb)—but not only done: it is performed.

Judgments are not only a set of rationally authoritative objects of knowledge and governance but are also the product of something that is done by living, breathing humans—and something, moreover, that is done in particular material or physical settings. To explore this a little, we shall first consider more fully the development of 'judgment' as a written or textual phenomenon by briefly telling the story of the emergence of law reporting (section 6.1). We will then consider the performance or theatre of the courtroom—the place of judgment (section 6.2)—before concluding the chapter by reflecting on the potentially complex relationships between the spoken or performed forms of judgment and its written record within the modern common law (section 6.3).

## 6.1 Tradition

Law was not always written down. The emergence of the common law as a written tradition can be traced at least as far as 1066, and the Norman conquest of England. Written methods of recording legal rules, as well as the decisions made in relation to them, existed before this time—the *Corpus Iuris Civilis*, mentioned in Chapter 1, is a good example of this. But it

DOI: 10.4324/9780429329784-6

was arguably with the Norman Conquest that one of the earliest and most important steps was taken on the journey towards today's written system of the common law. Here we will briefly trace aspects of how law emerged as a written phenomenon. Specifically, we will highlight the shift from oral practices to the written traditions in England that later spread across the common law jurisdictions of the world via British colonialism and was consolidated with the rise of the practice of law reporting.

We must begin by more fully noting the *Corpus Iuris Civilis*, for this is perhaps the earliest attempt to codify and record an entire legal system. It was compiled from pre-existing laws under the purview of the Roman emperor Justinian in the 6th century and also replaced those previous laws—indeed, they were supposedly destroyed after the *Corpus Iuris* was completed. In making sense of judgment, and particularly the way we normally access judgments today and understand the form that they take, this early encoding of law into a textual form is important to acknowledge. Via the large expanse of the Roman Empire, the effects of this legal document are widespread in Europe and thereafter via British colonialism across other parts of the world. It is often thought that the common law system of judgment and the written recording of adjudication is a divergence from Roman law. We mentioned this in Chapter 1, but the influence of Roman law, and of the *Corpus Iuris*, on the development of the common law as a specifically *written* form needs to be acknowledged in order to properly understand the apparent movement from oral to written judgment.

One of the main stories that was told about the common law is that it predated the Norman Conquest. When the Normans invaded and brought with them a system of law based upon written codes, the story goes that England ultimately did not adopt this system. Instead, the common law remained the core legal approach in England and Wales. However, this story was not really told until much later—with William Blackstone as its most famous proponent. The idea is that the common law retained its authority because it stemmed from 'time out of mind'—from the misty and ineffable annals of history. The common law had always been the law, and the role of the judge was to discover and make sense of this pre-existing set of principles and doctrines.

But this was not really the case: it is possible to trace the common law to historical influences, most notably the influence of 'invading' continental traditions and methods of encoding law into written text—of which the *Corpus Iuris* is emblematic. This is also true on the level of legal study and analysis, with 'invading' humanist methods of the Renaissance seeking to apply methods of historical and rhetorical analysis to the common law in order to understand its contingency and historical development, which we began to discuss in Chapter 3. It was in response to such a perceived threat to the authority of the common law that Blackstone was reacting when he clarified the idea that the common law had always been in existence and could trace its lineage to the dusty infinity of the past.

But even if Blackstone's romantic and somewhat unrealistic vision were correct, a key practical question remains: namely, how to access or trace the doctrines and authority of the common law. Recall the core of the common law method from Chapter 1: that like cases be treated alike, which results in *stare decesis* (precedent) and the irresolvable tension between individual cases and general rules from which 'settled' doctrines eventually develop. The assessing of the 'likeness' of different cases and, later, the communication of established principle and doctrine means that somehow decisions—judgments—need to be communicated. Oral communication was one way this could happen, but it is arguably not the most practicable given the scale and duration of law's operation across an entire civilisation. Ultimately, it is the written record of the judgment that becomes most important in the development of the common law, for this is the main practical way that decisions can be stored and shared for judges and legal subjects in the future.

Like with the *Corpus Iuris*, we are dealing here with encoding the law into a written form that supersedes or replaces the previous statement—in this case, the oral comments of the judge are replaced by the written record of those statements, which becomes authoritative precisely because it is understood to be such a record. Note that this does not reduce law to text: it is an observation that text has become one of the dominant ways through which law—whatever it might be—is accessed and administered. This also means that only those who are able to understand and work with texts—and the complex texts of law specifically—are able to access legal meanings.

But how did this written form come into being, and how does it actually work? If the judgments we access via WestLaw, Lexis, and other databases contain or communicate 'authoritative' judgments because of their connection with the judicial decision they record (and recall Chapter 2 on questions of authority), what actually is the nature of that connection? Before we can examine this and its complexities—which we will do in section 6.3, below—we need to briefly note how it came about (the rest of this section) and then to consider in more detail the nature of judicial speech itself (section 6.2).

One of the main things about the development of law reporting is that it was not done 'officially'—the legal profession was primarily responsible for undertaking law-reporting duties, and in many jurisdictions (including within the UK) this remains the case. Another is to understand the distinction between law reports and the court transcripts of judgments. We discussed this briefly in Chapter 1: court transcripts are the record of the judgment itself, as handed down or 'given' by the judge(s), and law reports are carefully curated and edited reproductions, with additional details and summaries, of the relatively small number of cases that actually change, develop, or clarify the law.

The judgments used for the most part by the legal profession are not those most closely connected to the judgment itself—as a speech or performance given by a judge in court—but are second-hand versions filtered through the procedures and editorial practices of law reporting. These processes are important for ensuring the efficient running of the profession because they help students of the law (from undergraduate to supreme court judge) to access, synthesise, and process the complexities of the common law, which otherwise would be quite unwieldy and opaque without significant time spent studying 'raw' or uncategorised court transcripts.

One of the earliest forms of law reports were the Year Books, which were not really law reports as we might think of them today, but rather a basic record of the 'pleas' argued in the 12th-century English royal courts, namely the Court of Common Pleas. The Year Books were not concerned with precedent but with communicating the complexities and techniques of argument in this most élite of judicial contexts. They were essentially textbooks or manuals, compiled by pleaders (advocates) for use by other pleaders and judges in navigating the oral argumentation of the Court. They were not relied upon as records or authority but of practice, and there were often multiple versions of the same case.

Skipping over centuries of details, these were followed by the Nominate Reports. The Nominate Reports were informal and made up of the personal notes from various legal professionals (judges, barristers, clerks, and so on) who each gave their name to their collection of reports (hence nominate). These were more concerned with recording precedent than technique but are of variable quality. While one of the earliest examples can be seen to have been published after some considerable effort at editing and a clear demarcation of commentary from the official legal decisions, most were published without editing and so are more like notes, resulting in really mixed standards of reliability.

Eventually, after some (failed) attempts to institute official law reporters, reports like those we might be familiar with emerged and were consolidated with the creation of the Incorporated Council of Law Reporting of England and Wales in 1865. There were more series of reports initially, but they have been gradually rationalised and reduced into the set of reports that England and Wales have today. With the development and sophistication of the law reports and their increasing reliability, the written tradition of the common law can be seen to flourish. The practical necessity of a law-reporting service for the efficient functioning of the legal system and profession produced the system we have today and a system that is largely shared across common law jurisdictions. To give a few examples, in England and Wales, the Incorporated Council of Law Reporters (ICLR) oversees law-reporting practices, with the Scottish Council of Law Reporting doing the same in Scotland, and Lexis doing so in Northern Ireland; in Australia, a range of private bodies produce law reports for the different federal states; in the United States many reports are now produced officially, with series at the federal level and from the Supreme Court, and Canada has a similar arrangement, with official reports from the different provinces of the country.

It is thus clear that the written tradition of the common law is a central feature of the legality and governance of Western states—but that this form is not a natural or given one. Underneath this textual edifice, the performative or oral tradition of law remains, as we shall explore in the next section.

## 6.2 Theatre

Law and judgment are not simply written documents. While there is a distinct and important textual dimension to legal judgment (see above and Chapter 5, and which we will explore again in Chapter 7 on interpretation), judicial procedures and decisions are not purely textual phenomena. Just thinking about a court makes this readily apparent: judgment is not only something written but also something passed or handed down—something done or performed by living beings within a particular context. The written judgment thus becomes somehow distinct from the performance of judgment, although still in some way connected to it—a complex relationship that we will examine in the next section (6.3). But the current section will give some details on the performative dimensions of judgment, ultimately drawing out its nature as theatre and as ritual.

In Chapter 2, we introduced the idea of the 'two bodies' of the sovereign, which is a way of thinking about the separation or continuity of the institutional office, or of state authority, with respect to the mortal limitations of the living people that inhabit those offices or administer that authority. One body of the sovereign is that of the living, breathing, dying monarch; the other is the mystical or immortal body of the sovereign as a symbol or pinnacle of power. This is a very useful concept, not just for understanding something of the relationships between individuals and the powerful institution of the state, but also in the particular context of judgment in a courtroom. Imagine a judge sitting in a court, all dressed up and ready for some intricate judicial action. He or she also, in quite a meaningful sense, has two bodies. One body, like the monarch, is that of a frail little human. The other is that of the judge: it is the representation of office, the emanation of state or legal authority, of institutional justice.

This distinction is not just conceptual; it is also expressed (or at least reflected) in the physical materiality of judicial practice: the frail human body clothed in the costume of the judge, of the office. Judicial robes and wigs are not practical things that help judges manage their paperwork—their function is distinctly symbolic. They are theatrical paraphernalia that make clear their authoritative status (and while this might not help with the paperwork, its symbolic function may have practical benefits in helping a judge manage their courtroom in an authoritative manner). Importantly, also, the costume of the judge is located within a whole host of theatrical and symbolic elements within a courtroom. Courtrooms all differ in various ways, but the separation (and often elevation) of the judicial bench from where lawyers, witnesses, parties, and observers sit is one consistent expression of the authority of the judicial office—it makes a space of power in which the human body of the judge places itself and performs its official functions.

The insignia and symbols of justice inside and outside courthouses also displays the institution of law and justice, serving important symbolic functions in a non-textual way. The architecture of court buildings also contributes to the performance of justice, as Linda Mulcahy makes clear in her studies of the architectural traditions of English courts. Mulcahy highlights the connections between the preferences for certain styles and the wider fashions in architecture during different historical periods. For example, the gothic edifice that is often associated with courthouses—imposing, powerful buildings, replete with spires and intricate decoration—is actually the product of particular trends at a particular time during the 18th century. During this period, the court system in England and Wales was expanding and becoming increasingly centralised. Courthouses were built in various urban areas to administer justice in those locations (previously, judges had travelled around the country, so only heard cases for limited periods of time in different places). The invocation of powerful architecture helped to secure the authority of these buildings and the justice they were seen to impose.[1] What this makes clear is that the exercise of judgment, its processes and effects, takes place not just in the spoken performance of the judge but also in the material setting within which that speech occurs.

These material features that surround judicial speech are all part of the phenomenon of judgment. Once we strip away the textual form of law reports, what remains is not the absence of law or simply a 'spoken' version of the judge's decision. Instead, a rich and complex ecosystem of signs and symbols can be seen: an aesthetics of the institution that plays various

---

1  See Linda Mulcahy, *Legal Architecture: Justice, Due Process and the Place of Law* (Routledge 2011), listed in the 'Further reading' section.

important roles in propping up judicial speech, turning otherwise normal words into spoken ritual, and thus into the performance of judgment. Ordinary words take on the quality of the institution and become words of law.

In this, in a sense, we can see 'two speeches': one being the ordinary spoken words of a mortal human; the other being the enduring words of law enshrined with the authority of the judicial office. Like the robes that clothe the mortal human in the office of judge, the full range of theatrical paraphernalia of the court process and institution 'clothes' the judge's words in the authority of law. The words spoken in the passing of judgment become words of law, an oral rendition of the norms, principles, doctrines, and rules of law, expressed and made perceptible to those who witness it.

This division between the mortal or everyday, and the enduring or institutional, also mirrors something we have already discussed in Chapter 1— the inherent tensions in common law judgment between specific cases and general rules. The rules of law, or the governance technologies of judgment (see Chapter 5), are applied to specific cases. In the practice of treating like cases alike, it is from specific cases that the general principles of the common law develop over time. Put in the context of what we have been discussing in relation to the aesthetics of the material theatre of judgment, it is through the particular and individual actions and decoration of people, and their mundane material settings, that the general or abstract power of the law or state (see Chapter 2) can be seen. The everyday elements of material forms, theatrical paraphernalia, and symbolic ritual are the specific cases or expressions through which the general power and authority of the law is maintained.

The distinction is in this sense the same: it is a distinction between the general and the individual. The 'two bodies' of the sovereign are reflected in the 'two bodies' of the judge, in the 'two speeches' of the judgment, it might be said even in the 'two architectures' of the courtroom (one mere crumbling masonry, the other a symbol of the enduring institution of law)— but also in the two bodies of the common law, one focused on resolving individual cases and the other with a trajectory that aims at the development of general rules and principles that transcend individual lives and events. And throughout, it is the materiality of the judicial process, its performance or theatre, that articulates these multiple 'bodies' or aspects of judgment.

## 6.3 Capture

The relationship between the recorded, or 'captured', judgment (in the court record or the law report) and the performative, or spoken, judgment that we have been discussing so far is complex. But if we recognise that the authority of a written judgment derives from the fact it is a record of a judgment produced or given during a formal judicial process (with the performance or ritual itself encountering all of the difficulties with respect to authority introduced in Chapter 2), then the various dimensions of this relationship—and its potential complexity—cannot be ignored.

One understanding of the relationship between spoken judgment (as performance, ritual, judicial process, etc.) and written judgment (as case report or court record) is that law reports are an unbiased and neutral record of the judgment handed down by the court. The written judgment is not the judgment itself but is evidence of the judgment—a copy of the words or reasoning 'captured' to enable future cases that are 'like' the one recorded to be treated in a like manner. Written judgments, as we have discussed above, are a practical tool to aid the common law to adhere to its central premise and thereby to achieve the justice that it is assumed that premise enables.

To record judgments in a practically accessible and enduring form (written documents) is to enable justice to take place across the slow burn of the common law. If lawyers and judges did not know what the judiciary had been deciding in cases for hundreds of years, or in the 1990s, or indeed last year or last week, it would not be possible to say with any confidence that like cases were being treated alike. On this level, written text is a practical way of ensuring justice is done. This is perhaps the most common assumption about law reports—and indeed such an assumption that it might be easily forgotten that the written documents are merely records of a judgment that takes place elsewhere and in a different form. But it is also an understanding of the relationship between performed and written judgments that overlooks some apparent problems

One is the practice of judges reading out only a summary of their judgment, with the full written document then only forming the court transcript or, in some cases, also being incorporated into the law reports. Indeed, it is not uncommon for those publishing law reports to give the judge final approval on the reported version. As noted above, different jurisdictions have different practices which give law reports a degree of official status or connection with the court or judge making the decisions. And all of these complicate the relationship between the written document and the ritual or formal court performance. These kinds of practices represent an interrelationship or a degree of back-and-forth with respect to the writing of the reported text, which undermines the simple assumption that the text 'captures' the judgment produced through the theatrical or performative process.

One response to this is to say that the production of the written record is part of the theatre, part of the process (indeed, we will encounter some more of this idea in Chapter 8 on rhetoric). This perspective would indicate that the court transcript or approved law report is not a record of the judgment given but is part and parcel of the decision itself—just not all of it. Indeed, to be encountered at all, as Peter Goodrich explains, the 'signs' of law:

> need their material support, the striation of the earth, the marking of a border, the inscription of a building, the printed text, the armorial flag or, most physically active of all, the speaker's elocution.[2]

Confining the signs we are concerned with merely to those of judgment, this means that the decisions that judges hand down are multimedia: the same judgment or decision is presented by the court in multiple forms, each or none of which are the 'official' or complete version. Some dimensions of the judgment are spoken, some are written, some are theatrically performed in other ways (e.g. through the architecture or ritual of the court)—but all are necessary, integrated elements in what we might term the 'assemblage' of judgment.

Pinpointing *the* judgment is thus tricky, if not impossible. There seems to be no single moment or object that we can comfortably say represents, contains, or actually *is* the judgment itself. All we actually have are a series of events and objects through or around which the idea(s) of judgment can be seen to coalesce or (as we explore in Chapter 7) legal interpretations can take place. The complex theatricality of the court process, the recording of a judge's decision, a judge's own drafting or co-production of the written arguments behind their decision, the editorial production of law reports with or without direct judicial input. No single one of these is *the* judgment or represents *the* source of the law, but through their performance and interplay, judgment is seen to occur or legal meanings to be articulated.

And so, finally, after the embodied or living theatre of the process is completed, once the court is adjourned and the law report is published and stored in libraries and databases across the jurisdiction—and beyond—what is left to endure, even after all the memories of the case and the judgment have dissipated or been taken to the grave, is the written record. These written documents thus become the trace of the complex process and theatre of judgment—the sediment of judgment that we students of the law disturb and excavate in an attempt to access the 'full' or 'real' judgment that has since dissipated (if it was ever identifiable). They become the dust of the common law. In part, it is to how these records are used and how these law reports and stored decisions are encountered and read that we turn in the next chapter—when we examine judgment as interpretation.

---

2  Peter Goodrich, *Advanced Introduction to Law and Literature* (Edward Elgar 2021) 42.

## 6.4 Further reading

- Also listed in Chapter 1, various materials and guides relating to the practice of law reporting can be found via the Incorporated Council of Law Reporting for England and Wales: <www.iclr.co.uk/knowledge/>.
- On the production and variable reliability of the Nominate Reports specifically, and Sir Francis Bacon's (failed) attempt to institute official law reporters, see John Baker, 'Law Reporting in England 1550–1650' (2017) 45 International Journal of Legal Information 209.
- On the architecture of courtrooms, see Linda Mulcahy, *Legal Architecture: Justice, Due Process and the Place of Law* (Routledge 2011). For a shorter example analysis, her paper on how the layout of the public gallery mediates questions of access to justice is a good start: Linda Mulcahy, 'Architects of Justice: The Politics of Courtroom Design' (2007) 16 Social and Legal Studies 383.
- For analysis of the role of silence within the theatre of the court, see Sean Mulcahy, 'Silence and Attunement in Legal Performance' (2019) 34 Canadian Journal of Law and Society 191. For a brief but more general engagement with some implications for engaging with law in terms of theatre, see Marett Leiboff, 'Theatricalizing Law' (2018) 30 Law and Literature 351. For a fuller and more advanced articulation of her ideas, Marett Leiboff, *Towards a Theatrical Jurisprudence* (Routledge 2019) should be consulted.
- Engagement with the visual appearance of judges, and the broader circulation of judicial images within, through, and around visual culture in general (from institution to popular culture), can be found in Leslie J Moran, *Law, Judges and Visual Culture* (Routledge 2021).

# 7  Interpretation

Hopefully, by now, it is clear that judgment is not a simple or uncontested matter and that there are many dimensions and questions involved in trying to understand how the law works in judicial contexts. The approaches discussed so far see judgment as reading the common law and applying it to the current case (Chapter 1) in an authoritative manner (Chapter 2), using various procedures or ways of thinking in order to undertake this application and arrive at a certain, practical outcome (Chapter 3), resulting in a body of judicial knowledge or 'truth' (Chapter 4), which is enabled by the technologies of its communication through text and language (Chapter 5) that have complex relationships with the performative or theatrical aspects of judicial decision-making (Chapter 6). But an issue not yet discussed directly, and one that arguably transcends or underlies a lot of the things discussed so far, is the question of interpretation.

Regardless of the authority, reason, technology, or performance of judgment, judges still have to read the law—to interpret or make sense of it—in order to provide judgment. Even if judgments are purely spoken or use technologies other than writing, future judges still need to make sense of those forms to understand the principles set down and treat similar cases in a similar manner. Judges and other students of the law need to understand what existing legal decisions might mean and how they are relevant to the present case. Here we will focus on the specifically interpretive nature of judicial decisions and thus of the common law as a whole. While questions of reasoning (Chapter 3) might seek to limit or authorise the practice of interpretation, this practice remains a necessary and unavoidable part of law that cannot be completely eradicated or predicted (see also Chapter 5 on automation and Chapter 9 on creativity).

The predominant form through which previous judgments are encountered is language, ultimately recorded in written law reports (see Chapters 5 and 6). The questions of interpretation we will focus on here are thus those relating to the interpretation of language and text, as opposed to interpreting,

DOI: 10.4324/9780429329784-7

for example, the ritual, symbolism, images, and so on that might be associated with judgment.[1] We will start by examining questions of the possibility of objective meaning (section 7.1) before looking at how the texts of law might produce meaning within its own structure (section 7.2), and finally concluding on the potentially violent nature of interpretation in the way it closes down alternative meanings (section 7.3).

## 7.1 Meaning

When a judge is faced with a case, her determination is made through the reading and application of existing law and principle—usually derived from the arguments and materials or citations presented to the court by the parties involved in the dispute. One important issue is thus whether written texts have single, objective meanings or not. When judges (and other students of the law) read the law, are they able to determine the actual or incontestable 'truth' of what that law means? The basic tension here is that between objectivism and subjectivism. Phrased starkly, objectivism holds that there is an objectively true meaning to a text, while subjectivism holds that any interpretation is subjective to the particular reading and context, and there is ultimately no single true meaning.

There are, of course, subtleties and nuances between these positions—for example, the true objective meaning might not necessarily be discovered but is aimed at as an ideal or is potentially there to be discovered with the right tools or insights (e.g. the correct mode of reasoning, as discussed in Chapter 3). Regardless of whether you think texts have objective meanings, the issue for judgment is how one determines whether an interpretation is 'correct' or not. How do we know when we have reached the 'correct' objectively true meaning, or which of the (subjective) interpretations available is the most just one?

Much of the interrogation of this question came out of a movement towards studying law by recognising that its written forms might, on at least one level, be understood as 'texts' in a similar way to other (non-legal) kinds of texts, such as literature or poetry. By acknowledging something of the 'reality' of judicial decision-making—that the written forms of judgment are not necessarily the judgment itself but instead are a recorded version of it (see Chapter 6)—we come to the question of the authoritative

---

1 Although these do remain important and, in many senses, encounter similar issues to those discussed here. An intrepid reader may be interested in exploring, for example, the visual modes of judgment: see Peter Goodrich, '*Imago Decidendi*: On the Common Law of Images' (2017) 1 Art and Law 1.

status of that text, and how we access the 'true' judgment itself, and how we read it legitimately as 'law' (rather than how we might read a novel or a cereal packet, for example). Rather than taking previous decisions as unquestionable statements of law, by recognising its need to be interpreted, written law can be understood as a genre of literature. This literary nature of law asks some quite radical questions about the nature of legal meaning and thus also the authority and techniques of the law itself as something mediated through written texts.

This approach to law significantly expands the methods available for legal study. Judgments and other legal texts become objects of study not just in terms of doctrinal coherence, their 'fit' or logic within the existing rules of law, or their practical or social effects, or their adherence to sound principles. Instead, the methods developed for studying literature and poetry can be applied. These methods focus on questions like the structure and rhetorical devices used in a text, on its constructed or created nature, on the contingency of its meaning and how it operates, of what a judgment might mean and how those meanings might be limited or problematic in the context of seeking just outcomes. These literary methods can also leave open the question of objective meaning or determining an outcome to a legal dispute, and aim instead at understanding how texts and written language work in a legal context.

In the context of judgment specifically, these kinds of questions can pose a radical challenge to the instinctive or assumed authority of written law reports since the subjectivism they seem to reveal unsettles the idea that law has the status of a unitary authority. If we can interpret using literary or poetic methods rather than legal or doctrinal ones, judges and lawyers are freed up to find all sorts of meanings within the texts they work with. Why does a judge need to follow precedent when she can reinterpret the law at will? To question whether the 'correct' meaning of law might be secured is disturbing for a legal institution that wishes to maintain judicial decisions as being in some way (objectively) valid, authoritative, or just.

We have touched on a version of this in Chapter 3, where we thought about judgments being validated through their particular modes of reasoning. In that chapter, we were thinking about unpicking the authority of law and how it secures itself through reasoned logic. Put in terms of interpretation, this becomes the more specific concern of whether the particular reasoning validates the *reading* of a legal provision that is being made. That is, whether we can claim that *this* interpretation (of a statutory section, judicial test, or common law principle) is the 'correct' one because it follows the correct procedures of logical reasoning, or that *this* interpretation is 'the best one' out of the range of possible subjective readings because it is the most rational in the context. But there are other possible ways of understanding how we might secure a 'correct' interpretation beyond the procedures of reasoning considered in Chapter 3, which we will introduce in the next section.

Before doing that, it is worth noting an idea that tries to explain the lingering authority of law and judgment, despite the fact it might be possible to subject it to a wide range of interpretations. This approach suggests that, while written documents might be interpreted in many different ways, when judges read case law, they are not interpreting freely. That is, judges do not just 'make up' their interpretation (see Chapter 9 on improvisation). Instead, judges are making their decisions in particular contexts and under the heavy weight of a long and strongly established history of judicial traditions and accepted methods of reading law. Judges interpret the law and seek to present acceptable readings within this context. As Stanley Fish puts it:

> Interpreters are constrained by their tacit awareness of what is possible and not possible to do, what is and is not a reasonable thing to say, and what will and will not be heard as evidence in a given enterprise; and it is within those same constraints that they see and bring others to see the shape of the documents to whose interpretation they are committed.[2]

Judges cannot simply interpret at will, because they are embedded within certain assumptions about how texts work and the methods that should be followed if their decisions will be accepted by the community of judges, the legal community in general, or the wider society in which they judge.

The set of methods that sitting judges might use are a contingent selection out of a much wider range of possible ways of reading; they are limited in scope by the practical and ideological contexts of the legal institution. Judicial meanings are thus judged correct or incorrect—just or unjust—based on the same standards that judges themselves use to read the law. In this version, the meanings of law are self-supporting and can be considered 'correct' within the cultural context of legal decision-making. Judges do not do what they want—they adhere, instead, to the normative and cultural expectations of what judges should do, of how judges should read. But this still begs the question of whether those privileged modes of interpretation are the best ones to use.

## 7.2 Text

The previous section introduced the idea that there is a range of possible ways of reading the law beyond the doctrinal and pragmatic methods

---

2 Stanley Fish, 'Working on the Chain Gang: Interpretation in Law and Literary Criticism' (1982) 9 Critical Inquiry 291, 211.

typically associated with legal practice and adjudication. In this section, we will briefly work through a selection of these, but first we must characterise the typical mainstream methods of legal reading. These are usually covered in introductory legal methods textbooks and cover approaches such as 'literal', 'purposive', and 'original' meanings of legal terms. The literal approach takes words at face value, in line with their dictionary definitions; the purposive approach reads words in light of what a provision or doctrine is trying to do and what its regulatory purpose is; and originalism tries to adhere to what a legal pronouncement would have meant at the time and in the context that it was originally made—often also connected to the intention of those who framed the legal text in question.

If we combine these restricted methods of reading with the principle of *stare decisis*, the dominant tradition of legal interpretation becomes apparent: it is to read the recorded history of judgments in a way that is as determinative as possible. It is in this way that the true or best interpretation can be achieved, rather than open-ended discussion of a wider range of meanings. We have seen something of this idea already, in Chapter 3, with Dworkin's concept of integrity: that judges (aim to) synthesise the complete history of the common law towards maintaining the best of all possible worlds—to reach (as an ideal) the single, correct interpretation. This, of course, doesn't really solve the interpretation question because what counts as the 'best world' has quite a scope for being understood in different ways.

But with respect to these dominant modes of legal interpretation, alternative reading methods are resisted or rejected. Speculative interpretations, or those not based on the kinds of reasoning typical of legal argument, or readings that draw on alternative sources outside of the record of decided cases, all operate as a challenge to law's ability to establish authoritative meanings. What we are dealing with here, basically, is the question of legal language.

One of the most prominent theories of how law's language works in recent decades is that of HLA Hart, who introduced a relatively basic conception from the study of linguistics into the study of law. He said that language has ambiguities in its ability to communicate meaning, and thus, because it uses language to communicate, there are interpretative grey areas involved in reading law. Luckily, most of the time meaning is clear due to convention, usage, and so on. Only in exceptional cases in law is meaning unclear or ambiguous, and it is these 'hard cases' where interpretive endeavour needs to be navigated.

Given the long history of linguistic study and the discipline of philology (the close study of texts) that existed at the time Hart was writing, this was not a particularly innovative or interesting observation. Indeed, it is symptomatic of a broader problem in legal understanding, which is 'straightforwardly to assert the existence of a social consensus as to meaning' that law rests upon, despite language clearly being very complex.[3] Yet Hart's claim was received as a radical shake-up of legal thought, bringing controversy in its seeming acceptance of indeterminacy of meaning and the potential for ambiguity within the texts of the common law.

In many ways, the value of Hart's work is that it (inadvertently) shows up the artificiality of the particular interpretative approaches that are seen as acceptable in law—an artificiality that other, later approaches sought to critique. In response to the perceived limitation in legal interpretation—and the claims that these methods were capable of producing 'true' or 'objective' meanings—the work of critical legal studies made a more radical claim. Critical legal studies emerged in the late 20th century in the US and sought to highlight the ambiguous and political nature of language not just in a limited range of 'hard cases' but as characteristic of *all* legal reading. Accordingly, while it is common for there to be a relatively strict delineation understood to exist between law and politics (it is assumed that judges make legal decisions on a technically legal basis that is removed from the vagaries of political debate), critical legal studies worked to uncover the inherently political nature of law.

A critical legal method does not seek to understand what a doctrine means 'objectively' or in its 'best' form but instead aims to uncover the ideology that it represents and the way judicial reading supports or maintains this ideology. This rests upon the acknowledgement that legal language is not just ambiguous in 'hard cases' but in its very linguistic or written form. In Chapter 5 (and then with the tradition of law reports in Chapter 6), we saw that law has become reliant on the technologies of written language—indeed, it is through its written form that law is able to be communicated over time, so judges can apply it in their present case. On one level, this written form embeds an inherent ambiguity into law and judgment and means that any determination, regardless of how it is secured as 'legitimate', represents one particular interpretation amongst many. Determining the meaning of any text involves an interpretation and thus the resolution of the inherent ambiguity of language. In the powerful and public contexts of law, this critical insight takes on political dimensions: legal meanings become debatable, with any outcome a particular choice of position among others and thus representative (consciously or not) of particular values and ideologies. In the context of the state powers that law generally operates, this means that any legal decision is also a political one.

---

3 See Peter Goodrich, 'Law and Language: A Historical and Critical Introduction' (1984) 11 Journal of Law and Society 173, 186.

The version of judgment that we inherit from such critical legal work is of the indeterminacy of language being navigated in the context of state power. The question of law's authority is no longer one of whether we can find a legitimate basis for a decision or for the law in general but something more concerned with the way (possibly illegitimate: see Chapter 2) power is embedded in the operation of legal language. Judgment, in this way of thinking, becomes an exercise of power over language: it is the meeting point of interpretation and authority.

The work of Jacques Derrida is important for framing this characteristic interaction of interpretation and authority we find in law and judgment. Derrida was not formally a lawyer, but he was very interested in the operation of language and the way texts are able to communicate meaning—especially in the contexts of power, where the meanings of texts were particularly important. Derrida's insights are wide-ranging, but one of his most central claims was about what he called 'grammatology'. This idea encounters the inability of finding a single, legitimating source for the meaning of a text. Instead of the commonly understood notion that words or signs 'carried' meaning (e.g. due to their conventional or arbitrary associations with particular objects, meanings, or concepts), grammatology argues that language systems are wholly internal. Meaning is not found by referring to something outside of language (an object or idea) but instead is a product of the complex interrelation of all the associated elements within the system(s) of language itself. 'Dog' does not mean dog because it refers to an actual dog or the idea of a dog in general but instead because of its systemic relationships with other inscribed words and signs that are not 'dog' but help determine what 'dog' means, by being closely connected to it (e.g. hairy, paws, cat, tail, woof, etc.) or contrastingly distinct (e.g. infinitesimal, tricycle, puppet, cheesecake, etc.).

Importantly, meaning is only derived from the written inscriptions that we can actually encounter—a focus on what is actually written, as indicated by the term 'grammatology' as the close study of written forms. It is the complex web of written signs that produces or supports meaning. There is no absolute or ultimate meaning or source that we can access or point to; instead, meaning emerges in the complex interaction of textual elements. It is a form of radical materialism, which results in an expansive sea of associations to be explored in the elaboration of possible meanings. In Derrida's ideas, meanings multiply as we trace the connections and linkages between the signs that make up our interconnected systems of meaning—and this expands further when it is appreciated that Derrida's understanding of text or writing is one of inscription understood in its broadest sense (not just written words but any kind of material mark or trace).

The significance of this theory for law is perhaps quite obvious once we reframe the quest for meaning as the quest for authority (since a meaning is only 'correct' in law if it has the requisite authority as law). In trying to determine the authority of a law, of an interpretation or decision, judges point to previous cases as 'sources of law'. But in Derrida's formulation, the ultimate source remains elusive—we can trace one source to another, trying to find where the trail ends and the foundation of legal legitimacy rests, but this search is never-ending (see Chapter 2). It is the web of law, the mutual interrelation of the different parts of a legal system or sets of rules, that supports the activities of judgment and legal determination. There is no final, concrete source to be found.

One of Derrida's examples is the US Constitution, often understood as a foundational document—we can at least trace the authority of a law report back to that jurisdiction's constitutional document, surely? Perhaps, but what is the source of authority for the constitutional document itself? Since this document creates the legal system, there is necessarily no law prior to its existence, meaning it had no legal authority to come into force in the first place.

With Derrida, we arguably reach a point at which texts—including judicial texts—appear to have little or no secure meaning. Indeed, the ideas of postmodernism or poststructuralism, often associated with Derrida and thinkers like him, is sometimes resisted or rejected by those working in law. Such ideas of the relativity of meaning, of the absence of a discoverable legitimating source, are seen as too unhelpful or impractical. These ideas radically undermine the judicial project of finding the 'true' meaning of law and making decisions in practical contexts, opening meanings up instead of helping to close them down. It is to this theme of the 'closing down' or securing of meanings within a context of their potential openness that we shall turn in the final section of this chapter, framed in terms of the violence of judgment.

## 7.3 Violence

Critics of Derrida might point out that there is political authority for the founding document of legal jurisdiction; that is, it is the democratic will of the people to put it in place. But if this is so, what is the law that underpins that democratic process and legitimates it, if the constitution is not yet in force? Derrida's point is that the founding of such a system must be understood as an exercise of force (that is, violence)—a primary imposition of law without any prior authority to legitimate it. But more than this, that this instigating force or violence of foundations is repeated in each interpretive act, in each exercise of judgment. This is, perhaps, a counter-intuitive idea to those used to thinking of law as a largely benevolent (albeit flawed) institution, so we will examine it in a little detail in this final section of the chapter.

The core idea here is closure. As we've just seen, in interpreting the law—in making sense of what the history of case law and the words of statutes might mean—judges work through the available inscriptions and their associations, with their analysis arguably limited or shaped by the conventions of the institution or by the supposedly 'correct' methods of reasoning discussed in Chapter 3. In making a judgment, a conclusion or interpretation is reached, and a decision is made. And it is precisely this movement that can be considered violent or as representative of the violence of judgment or the repetition of the founding violence of law itself.

The dominant movement in judgment is to resolve or end a dispute or conflict (see Chapter 1). Once we recognise that this is necessarily mediated through language in some way and thus comes with the baggage of needing to be interpreted, a tension opens up between the desire to close down meaning and come to a conclusion (e.g. X is guilty, Y broke the contract, this statutory section means Z) and the quality of language as opening up to uncertainty or being unable to be decided through the potential multiplication of meanings (e.g. what do the terms of this offence or contract mean, how do we limit their meaning, what else is relevant to consider—what Derrida calls 'the undecidable'). Under Derrida's model, in particular, we can interpret endlessly. Because the signs we use to communicate (words, inscriptions) gain their meaning from their interconnection with other related signs, meaning can always be reframed or reinterpreted by associating or connecting signs in different ways. That is, law tries to close down meaning, but language always works to open it up.

When judges deliberate and interpret and work towards their decisions, they engage in this opening up, and Derrida says this is required if a judgment is to be just.

> Each case is other, each decision is different and requires an absolutely unique interpretation, which no existing, coded rule can or ought to guarantee absolutely. At least, if the rule guarantees it in no uncertain terms, so that the judge is a calculating machine—which happens—we will not say that he is just, free and responsible.[4]

If a judge mechanically applied the previous rules or cases without deliberation, it would not be a responsible decision, primarily because it would not be able to take anything of the specifics of the present case into account. Judgment, to be just, therefore must risk indecision: 'A decision that didn't

4 Jacques Derrida, 'Force of Law: The "Mystical Foundation of Authority"' (1990) 11 Cardozo Law Review 919, 961.

go through the ordeal of the undecidable [i.e. potentially infinite deliberation] would not be a free decision, it would only be the programmable application or unfolding of a calculable process'[5] (and see Chapter 5 for issues of programming judgment to be automatic).

In order to make a just decision, we must open up meaning and explore its potentially infinite pathways that language and inscription make available to us. We will explore this idea a little more in Chapter 9, on the improvised nature of judgment, but the point here is that judgment (properly understood) always moves into a space of infinite potential. This potential is required; otherwise, there is no prospect for a just decision. We must open to the possibility of finding the 'correct' or 'best' or 'just' outcome; otherwise, we will not be able to find it at all.

But this deliberation, this exploration and analysis of potential meanings and interpretive outcomes, must necessarily come to an end. A decision cannot be just unless it has actually been made: parties must get an answer, conflicts must be resolved, a case must have an outcome. The practical exigencies of adjudication always force the potentially infinite deliberations to come to a premature end. Premature because the outcome is always determined before everything can be considered. Indeed, it is impossible for everything to be considered—so this somewhat arbitrary or forced end to analysis and deliberation is always embedded in every decision. Every judgment is made before it is ready, its interpretations cut off before they can be completed (in mechanical or automatic judgments, before they have even properly started). A decision can thus never be 'just', according to Derrida, because if it has been made, it has necessarily closed down the potential for just meaning to be found. In this model, justice is always something we are aiming for, that must be aimed for, but remains something that is always in the future and is never reached.

Judgment, in this model, is always violent—an exercise of arbitrary or unjustified force. In coming to a point and determining an outcome, judgment operates along one of two alternative lines. Either, firstly, as a mechanical application of previous law that is thus unable to consider the specifics of the case under consideration, and thus does violence to the parties before it by not properly seeing or representing them. Or, secondly, as an arbitrary assertion of meaning without full justification because an ultimate source of authority for an interpretation is not possible within the expanding structure of language. In terms of interpretation, judgments assert—mechanically or without prior legitimacy—particular meanings for texts in the face of their inherent potential to be understood differently.

5  Derrida (n 4) 963.

## 7.4 Further reading

- For Hart's articulation of law as a generally clear system of linguistic rules, as part of a larger theory of positive law, see HLA Hart, *The Concept of Law* (2nd edn, Clarendon 1997).
- On the idea of legal interpretation being shaped and limited by judicial convention or culture, see Stanley Fish, 'Working on the Chain Gang: Interpretation in Law and Literary Studies' (1982) 9 Critical Inquiry 201. A fuller presentation of the idea of 'interpretive communities' can be found in Stanley Fish, *Is There a Text in This Class? The Authority of Interpretive Communities* (Harvard University Press 1980).
- For an up to date overview of the study of law and literature, in particular exploring the distinct genre of judicial writing, see Peter Goodrich, *Advanced Introduction to Law and Literature* (Edward Elgar 2021). On the slow reading and opening up of legal texts, in contrast with law's dominant mode of reading for closure and certainty, see Peter Goodrich, 'Slow Reading' in Peter Goodrich and Mariana Valverde (eds), *Nietzsche and Legal Theory: Half-Written Laws* (Routledge 2005).
- The main text in which Derrida engages with law is Jacques Derrida, 'Force of Law: The "Mystical Foundation of Authority"' (1990) 11 Cardozo Law Review 919, but other of his legally relevant texts include: Jacques Derrida, 'Archive Fever: A Freudian Impression' (1995) 25 Diacritics 9; Jacques Derrida, 'Before the Law' in Derek Attridge (ed), *Acts of Literature* (Routledge 1992); and, his main work on deconstruction, *Of Grammatology* (Gayatri Chakravorty Spivak tr, John Hopkins University Press 1974).
- There is much written on Derrida and the law, and I cannot begin to comprehensively list it here. Instead, a few examples. For commentary and analysis of Derrida's 'Before the Law', see William E Conklin, 'Derrida's Kafka and the Imagined Boundary of Legal Knowledge' (2016) Law, Culture and the Humanities, DOI: 10.1177/1743872116660778. On Derrida's reception by the legal academy in general, see Peter Goodrich, 'Europe in America: Grammatology, Legal Studies, and the Politics of Transmission' (2001) 101 Columbia Law Review 2033. And on deconstruction as a mode of reading case law, see for example Chris Lloyd, '"*Ce Qui Arrive*": Deconstruction, Invention and the Legal Subject of *R v R*' (2012) 37 Australian Feminist Law Journal 65.

# 8  Rhetoric

In everyday understanding, if something is 'rhetorical', it is usually associated with being empty or meaningless (such as political rhetoric in lieu of real promises or action) or just for effect (such as a rhetorical question). In this way, rhetoric is often seen to sit in contradiction to real substance or meaning. But in essence, rhetoric is about the way something is presented or communicated—it is about how a 'message' meets an 'audience'. This encompasses things like the 'lies' of politicians (as a message without substance, thus 'mere' rhetoric), but it also covers the way other messages are communicated. The study of rhetoric, in fact, is a rich philosophical discipline that works to understand how meaning works. The previous chapter indicates how important this might be for law and judgment (not to mention human communication in general) and thus how alternative insights into the question of law's 'meaning' might be helpful in better understanding how judgment works.

In this chapter, we will consider the way some aspects of judgment can be understood through the notion of rhetoric. We will start in section 8.1 by considering who the 'audience' of legal judgment might be (such as the parties to a case, lawyers, other judges, undergraduate students, the public, people in the future, and so on). In section 8.2, we will turn to the argumentative nature of judgment as something that seeks to persuade its audience and how rhetoric is important with respect to that aim. In the final section (section 8.3), we will consider the constructed nature of judgment that engagement with its rhetorical forms reveals.

## 8.1 Audience

Who is judgment for? More specifically: to whom does the common law communicate? If the law is for everyone (i.e. no one is above the law), then the question of law's audience is meaningless—it speaks to everyone and thus has no specific identifiable audience. Any meaningful question

DOI: 10.4324/9780429329784-8

of 'audience' must instead be a matter of who actually witnesses or reads it in practice. The common law has relied heavily not only on its written forms of communication but also on controlling who is authorised to use or interpret those texts—who holds the required office. The practices of communicating the law are thus of central importance in understanding not only how meaning might work in the contexts of judgment but also the potential for the common law to remain exclusive or inaccessible to significant proportions of the population.

It may be that no one is above the law, but it is also the case that not everyone has equal access to the law—in terms of 'access to justice' issues as much as being able to navigate its means of communicating. Indeed, these are strongly linked when it is remembered that lawyers and legal representatives serve in large part as professional interpreters between their clients and the technical systems of law. Without the ability to access representation, the 'people's' access to the law may be severely limited. Put in another (perhaps more cynical) way, the existence of lawyers—and the fees they charge—depends upon the *in*accessibility of law for a general audience of legal subjects. If everyone could read and understand the law, if it was simple and clear and certain, lawyers would be out of a job.

There are thus a number of groups which might be identified as the practical audience of judgment: the parties in the case, but perhaps only through the interpretation of their counsel, or only in part; the lawyers in the case, of course, but also lawyers in general who use judgments as 'authorities' for future arguments and, similarly, the community of judges. Other audience groups might include the press, should there be sufficient interest, or academic commentators, or—if they can access it via court records or a public database, for example—armchair enthusiasts and the public at large. But on a practical level, these latter groups are arguably secondary: judgment speaks first to the community of legal experts and practitioners who have to work with the record of that judgment and who are sufficiently trained to interpret and apply it in an appropriate or legitimate manner. Judgments may speak to the public ideologically or in general terms, and arguably must do so in order to be considered 'law' (see Chapters 1 and 2), but their technical legal aspects speak primarily to other students of the law (undergraduates, practitioners, judges).

Nevertheless, judgments do bind society as a whole, and so their quality as public communication cannot be ignored. The critical question is the way this communication might be accessed or filtered through the legal profession in various ways. If we recall some of the aspects of judgment from previous chapters, we can see how the question of audience can play into these in different ways in terms of the rhetorical effects they might have. For instance, the public communication of judgment is perhaps less about the technical legal substance than about the general power, authority, and grandeur of the legal institution. These dimensions are seen in the visual, procedural, and architectural rhetoric attached to the performative rituals of judicial decision-making. Legal decisions are not made in any old place but only in specific and controlled institutional locations embedded amongst complex protocols and procedures.

In Chapter 6 we considered the performative aspects of judgment. And indeed, to consider judgment as a type of performance is clearly to consider some of its rhetorical aspects: a performance, in its theatrical quality, is overtly concerned with the way it appears to or 'meets' its audience. Thus, in the judicial context, these rhetorical features are most obviously things like institutional architecture and dress, as well as the adherence to ritual and tradition. Reframed as rhetoric, these aspects take on a strongly symbolic or emblematic quality. It is these elements that most publicly display the institution of law and the 'face' of judgment, most directly communicating law's general authority. The theatre of judgment is part of the way it secures its legitimacy in the public eye through the psychological, symbolic, and emotional effects that its forms evoke in the public imagination.

These symbolic features of the rhetorical appearance of judgment connect strongly with the general or abstract quality of the common law rather than the specifics of individual cases. The spectacle of judgment speaks of law's universal power, its connection with the right to govern, and with the divinity or tradition that traditionally underpins legal authority (see Chapter 2). Indeed, by 'staging' something of law's divine connection, its authority is secured in the hearts and minds of legal subjects, and much of this staging is done through the rhetorical features of institutional appearance. Robes, wigs, court layouts, architectural decoration, sacred rituals of procedure, tradition from time out of mind—all these performative aspects from Chapter 6 contribute to the rhetorical separation of the mundane words or individuals of the legal system from a higher sense of justice or divine authority, turning human decisions into authoritative and binding legal pronouncements.

Although primarily speaking to an untrained public audience, these features are also received by lawyers and judges, as well as individual parties in specific cases, helping to maintain the binding nature of a judge's decision and the authority of the court to which lawyers must show deference when making submissions on behalf of their clients. But for these audiences, judgment has other rhetorical aspects to consider. These relate to more technical dimensions, such as the particular use of sources, reasoning, and procedure. Even once the veil of theatrics is lifted, you might say, there are important rhetorical features that seek to secure judgment for these 'initiated' audiences. We will explore these dimensions across the remainder of this chapter.

## 8.2 Form

Combined, the theatrical and technical rhetoric of judgment present society with a powerful and binding institution of justice. The significance of this can be seen, for example, if the way judicial processes handle evidentiary questions of fact. Instinctively, it might be assumed that 'facts' are simple and unquestionable things—it is the 'reality' of what has happened or of something that exists. But as discussed in Chapter 4, the knowledge we have of the world is actually the product of particular processes of knowledge production or method. The most dominant of these is science. But science does not simply point to the world and transparently present the 'truth' of things: it has its own particular processes and methods through which 'facts' are determined. Through the scientific method—i.e. controlled, repeatable experimentation—hypotheses are tested, and 'facts' are secured, albeit conditionally and always open to reform or change as more testing and evidence takes place across time (scientific knowledge now is different from one hundred years ago, for example). Law follows a similar structure, whereby facts are produced through judicial processes—as we discussed in Chapter 4. Put in terms of rhetoric, what we think of as true (in science as much as in terms of legal evidence or the facts of a case) is that which we can be convinced of as truth. Science has a powerful rhetorical form for convincing various communities of the nature and structures of the world, and legal processes similarly act to authorise or underwrite the 'legal truth' of evidence.

Put in this way, the importance of rhetoric becomes vast for, in some sense, it is rhetoric that enables us to know anything beyond our own personal experiences and for communal or collective knowledge to exist at all. When we shift concern away from fact towards the more obviously contested concept of justice, then the rhetorical features become more overt—it is via certain procedures and displays, following authorised submissions and debate, that the legal institution, via its judgments, is able to produce (or perform) just decisions.

We have examined already some of the ways in which judgments can be seen to secure their authority or legitimacy. Be it through the use of particular modes of reasoning and argumentation, through the spectacle of office. Taking a slightly different perspective on these strategies, we can also frame them in terms of rhetoric. What matters in the use of judicial reasoning, or in the appropriate use of argumentation and the logical unfolding of analysis, is not just the way those methods might approach objectivity or fairness. What matters, also, is the way these methods might be seen to approach—or even achieve—objectivity and fairness.

To reason and explain one's basis for a decision, to apply particular modes of argumentation and logic, also has a rhetorical function. It transmits a legitimacy along with the decision. A judge does not just give an outcome but also shows her working. If the purpose of using particular methods of judicial reasoning was simply to secure justice through their operation, the explanation would not strictly be necessary. The communication of the reasons along with the decision thus serves an additional function: to shore up the judicial institution and its decisions against accusations of illegitimacy, arbitrariness, or bias—of injustice.

In part, this rhetorical form satisfies the requirement for justice to be public and, in this sense, can be said to serve a function that is not simply rhetorical. Note how the potential removal of this aspect in automated judgments might undermine the legitimacy of judgment, as discussed in Chapter 5. By publishing the reasons for the decision, those reasons are exposed to scrutiny and oversight—by the community of lawyers and judges as well as the public and society being governed. But this function itself is part of the wider rhetorical features of law: the institution or administration of law secures its legitimacy, its status *as law*, through opening itself up to public scrutiny. In this sense, it is a rhetorical move—a move concerned with its transmission or communication, with how the 'law' is encountered or received by its community of subjects.

One way to understand this rhetorical dimension is perhaps as an envelope that contains or wraps around the more substantive concerns. The validity of the specific reasoning in a case or the procedures of public scrutiny can be seen to help work towards the fairness of law—for example, by ensuring the common law method of treating like cases alike is adhered to or by ensuring that decisions are rationally defensible. But underpinning these important dimensions is a desire for law to be accepted as legitimate, to be able to regulate, for without that acceptance, law cannot operate. The wider need for public legitimacy is, of course, a distinctly political question. Hence, through this rhetorical dimension, the political dimensions of judgment can be seen. The state constantly works to maintain its acceptance, and in the legal context, this is understood as the social reception of institutional law, of the state's governmental technologies and methods (see Chapter 5) as legitimate. Without this acceptance, the state cannot secure or maintain its powerful position. In this way, law and judgment exist as species of political rhetoric.

The common law method of treating like cases alike is part of the rational or logical methods through which the common law maintains its (apparent) fairness and legitimacy. Public scrutiny is part of this: we must be able to *see* that this is taking place. And this requires the citation of previous cases to which the current case can be compared to ensure likeness is being adhered to (or not found). Accordingly, judicial arguments are not just the product of reasoning and logic; there are also more material features to law's rhetorical dimensions, namely the use of sources and written technologies. Thus, when we look at a law report, we see a whole lot of text. Text that seeks to capture or communicate the serious reasoning of the judge, its reasonableness and validity measured against the standards within the community of judges and lawyers. But also, a text that is filled with citations—mostly of previous cases. The appearance of the written form of judgment can be termed intertextual: it is compiled and constructed from fragments and extractions from legal decisions and the words of statutes (and sometimes other acceptable texts, such as leading textbooks or, occasionally, academic research). We might call this the judicial *style*, or the characteristic traits of legal judgment as a genre of writing, and it is through this intertextual style that judgment crafts its messages for the legal community.

This appearance of legal documents echoes the structures of the common law: firstly, the principle of treating like cases alike; secondly, the irresolvable tension between the general and the particular, between the abstract rule and the individual case. Citation and intertextuality fulfil both of these key characteristics. As we discussed in Chapter 1, these elements are closely related—with the fact of treating like cases alike in many ways giving rise to the generalised form of legal rules and pronouncements. Thus, the citation of previous cases serves an important rhetorical function: it shows the audience of the judicial text that preceding cases are being considered, that *stare decisis* is being respected and that 'likeness' is in play—one way or another. (The content of the reasoning and analysis, of course, could always dispel this appearance, and thus the importance of reasoning and form of logic that was discussed more fully in Chapter 3 should not be forgotten—but here it is placed as part of the rhetorical features of judgment.)

The second dimension is also reflected: in the simple fact of citing legal sources. By summoning or recalling existing general rules, principles, and doctrines, the judicial text makes apparent that the decision is being made in the context of the general rules. By calling forth general laws in the context of an individual case, discussing 'settled' principle alongside the specifics of the case—by applying the law to the facts—the structure of judicial documents necessarily oscillates between the general and the particular. In these terms, there is perhaps a no better way for the common law to rhetorically display itself. The intertextual form of legal discussion and its reporting does much of the work of displaying that the discussion is a legitimate part of the common law.

With this consideration of the intertextual quality of judicial decisions, we have crossed a boundary from content to material form. The material (performative or documentary) nature of judgment is often overlooked or disregarded as irrelevant with respect to the *content* of the law. But the material form of judgment, as we have just seen, is important in how it communicates its message—how the law is encountered—with the potential to shape access to and interpretation of the 'settled' law of previous cases. We discussed the performative aspects of judicial theatre—an important dimension of its material appearance—in Chapter 6, and that discussion can now clearly be seen to fall within an understanding of judgment as having significant rhetorical qualities. In Chapter 6 we also looked at issues with judgment being 'captured' in documentary form. And for nearly all students of the law, it is the final written document of a judgment that is most centrally encountered—be it in court record or law report—and is cited as part of the intertextual rhetoric of judicial discourse. On a material level, then, judicial decisions arguably appear today most overtly as documents, and documents full of citations.

## 8.3 Contingency

Knowledge and truth are those things that we are able to be convinced of as true. Science has the scientific method to do this, producing authoritative knowledge about the empirical world through repeatable, controlled experimentation. And this method is out in the open: it is commonly acknowledged and part of mainstream scientific discourse, and thus, it is one that is potentially open to question and to revision or could be placed alongside alternatives as just one method amongst many. Indeed, that openness is perhaps part of its apparent robustness—for problems or limitations can be pointed out.

Compared to science, law can be said to up the ante in the authority stakes. Law goes a step further: rather than openly relying upon a robust method, law presents itself as lacking any underlying rhetorical procedure or form. Law is not performance; law is not argumentation or interpretation—law simply *is*. Performance, documents, argument, reason, ritual, interpretation—these are the strategies by which law and judgment work to efface their rhetorical nature and thus try and shed any suspicion of contingency or non-objectivity.

Law comes from somewhere else: it exists separate from culture, society, and politics, over which it has effects as a regulatory force. This is an understanding of law that runs through much of legal thought and serves to prop up or maintain law's authority. If law is to be authoritative, it must be absolute and lack contingency—otherwise, it is up for debate, questionable, and its regulatory force unravels. We have examined a number of strategies that judgments employ to maintain their authority so far in this book—from connections to some 'source' of authority (Chapter 2), to reasonable methods and rational logic (Chapter 3), to technological forms that resist questioning (Chapter 5) or require sophisticated expertise to understand and use

(Chapter 7), to performative rhetoric that presents the appearance of authority (Chapter 6 and above in this chapter). The question of law's authority can thus be seen to be a fraught one, and one that is perhaps complex and ultimately irresolvable. But with rhetoric, we can access an important understanding of the question of law's authority that recognises the way these difficulties are sidestepped or avoided.

By avoiding the question of law's legitimacy, law is allowed to function on a practical level without its authority disappearing. The key strategy that law employs to this end is to deny its contingency. As a form of rhetoric, law presents itself as something that lacks origins, that is not contingent upon human artifice. This is a process known as reification—law is reified into an objective form, free from the contingencies and questionable biases inherent in human creativity and construction. It is quite common in popular understandings for law to be treated in this way—as something unquestionable, as 'just the way it is'. The rule of law is a good example here—especially in the context of rhetoric and politics. The 'rule of law' is a term that gets used in lots of different contexts and to lots of different ends, but in its most general sense, perhaps means something like always adhering to the law, to the rules that the law underwrites or contains or is made up of. But moreover, that law is itself rules—that law is supreme and authoritative. The rule of law thus represents the idea that the law is not to be applied unevenly, with some being able to escape its provisions or effects. Another phrase to this effect is 'no one is above the law'. In these common (and perhaps common sense) understandings—adopted by lawyers, politicians, and back-seat commentators alike—one finds a leading example of the idea of law as existing 'out there' somewhere, from where it binds or regulates our lives. It is above us all and comes down to intervene in our lives 'from beyond'.

If the law 'rules', if no one is above it, then it can be invoked to have real effects and be applied to regulate, control, or limit specific instances of conduct. An individual cannot simply kill another; someone cannot go back on a bargain—'the law' oversees human conduct and can intervene as a powerful institution. By looking at the rhetorical dimensions of the legal institution, the question of law's authority is reframed. Legal authority becomes a product of certain signs and symbols, certain ways of speaking or presenting knowledge or value. Law is not 'out there' but is the product of the relations between the institution and its subjects—between the state and its audience. To see judgment as rhetoric is to locate its regulatory force and authority in its representation, in its means of communicating and theatrical performance, in the moment when legal speech meets those whom it claims to bind.

Here is an abridged passage from Peter Goodrich's early work on law's rhetoric, in which he sets out the key rhetorical features of legal discourse—some of which, such as the use of citation, we have already noted and expanded upon above. In this passage, he is focused on how law's broad rhetorical features contribute to its reification. For our purposes, it is thus worth quoting at length:

> Legal discourse presents itself as a context-independent code, as the authoritative elaboration of the logical entailments of a distanced and obscure language system . . . Legal discourse is pre-eminently *prior* discourse, a discourse that is already 'written' and requires only the addition of the passive philological techniques of reinvocation . . . its vocabulary is correspondingly governed by doctrines of memory, recognition and usage, defined in textual terms by reference to . . . inert and calcified meanings and procedures, and finally by an epistemology . . . of the 'sources' of law in which words are transmitted by a dogmatics of quotation, reference, citation and specialised and restricted commentary—the techniques, in short, of a textual repetition which disavows the relevance of the lives and commitments of its rhetoricians to the monologic symbolic usages which they discover and declare.[1]

In less words, law's rhetoric of distance and citation hides the social origins of its language and the human origins of its decisions. If law is simply 'out there', lost in the dusts of time in the history of the common law, inaccessible or impenetrable by its subjects, the activity of judges becomes an act of discovery and application—of memory and usage, in Goodrich's terms. The previous law binds the judge, and they mechanically or dogmatically apply what was decided previously.

Hopefully, from the discussion so far in this book, you can appreciate that this 'mechanical application' model is problematic on a number of levels—and rhetoric gives us a new angle on this. Law is not simply applied but is written or produced through certain argumentative practices and material signs and forms—'monologic' ones, as Goodrich criticises. The activity of judgment, even where a judge may think they are mechanically bound to a particular interpretation or application, is a rhetorical one. It is the production of a performance and the creation of a trace or inscription kept on record for future judges. James Boyd White classically articulated this in his observation that, whenever we communicate, we imagine both ourselves and our audience—and the way we imagine affects the way we communicate. He goes as far as stating that even the processes of legal reason and

---

1 Peter Goodrich, 'Law and Language: An Historical and Critical Introduction' (1984) 11 Journal of Law and Society 173, 188–189.

analysis themselves (if done 'properly') are captured within an understanding of judgment as a mechanical activity:

> True reasoning meets the standards of an intellectual machine. Its parts fit together to work in ways that can be rendered wholly explicit in language, which is of course another machine . . . Once a choice of value is made, law is simply a system of implementation.[2]

But, and this is White's key point, we can imagine law in a different way—and doing so can improve our understanding of law and judgment or open it up to new possibilities for critical engagement. As White says:

> To imagine law as rhetorical . . . is to think of it not as a machinelike process of cause and effect, driven by a rationality that is fundamentally instrumental in kind, but as a discourse maintained by the processes of persuasion and argument. These processes work not simply by ends-means rationality but by all the movements of mind and feeling that lawyers and judges display.[3]

By hiding its rhetorical quality, in being imagined as a machine, law becomes unquestionably true and authoritative, the inexorable activity of a predictable system. In this version, our task as students of the law thus becomes one of learning the parts of the system and how they work, with our own agency and understanding—our own rhetorical activity—being forgotten or suppressed. Taken seriously, this understanding means that the argumentative practices that sustain the discourse of law are hidden or denied, and the creative and analytical art of the lawyer or judge—their exclusive proficiency with texts, language, logic, conceptualisation—are reduced to an (ultimately predictable) algorithm (see Chapter 5 again on automation).

Unpacking or even merely acknowledging the rhetorical dimensions of judgment—as we have begun to do in this chapter—opens law up to its constructed nature. We have seen a few ways in which the technologies of written language operate not only to enable the communication of law but also as a means of securing authority—for example, by placing law 'elsewhere' or by maintaining exclusive control over the meanings of regulatory texts through official processes of judgment. It can thus be seen that the turn

---

2 James Boyd White, 'Imagining the Law' in Austin Sarat and Thomas R Kearnes (eds), *The Rhetoric of Law* (University of Michigan Press 1996) 34.

3 White (n 2) 37–38.

to rhetoric punctures the hermetic safety of a ruling élite who control the meanings of law's textual forms and other institutional signs.

Importantly, this need not cause the downfall or collapse of the legal institution. Instead, it gives us a richer, more informed capacity for understanding and critiquing the operation of state power through the assemblage of judgment. It opens up to a fuller ability to engage with the practices and values that are embedded in law, judgment, and judicial theatre, to better understand the reasons for a decision, of the values or ideology it represents, the way it is shaped for an audience, and the limitations that particular methods place upon the regulatory and juridical capacity of the state institution.

## 8.4 Further reading

- For an introductory overview of legal rhetoric, in particular its rhetoric of hiding its rhetorical form, see Peter Goodrich, 'Rhetoric and Modern Law' in Michael MacDonald (ed), *The Oxford Handbook of Rhetorical Studies* (Oxford University Press 2014).

- For analysis of law's use of 'backgrounding' in its everyday forms, see Illan rua Wall, 'The Ordinary Affects of Law' (2019) Law, Culture and Humanities DOI: 10.1177/1743872119886509. Extended analysis of the materiality of law and the way it 'hides' its contingency in order to create an atmosphere of legitimate authority can be found in Andreas Philippopoulos-Mihalopoulos, *Spatial Justice: Body, Lawscape, Atmosphere* (Routledge 2015).

- On how the way we imagine law changes our understanding of it and exposes its rhetorical assumptions, see James Boyd White, 'Imagining the Law' in Austin Sarat and Thomas R Kearnes (eds), *The Rhetoric of Law* (University of Michigan Press 1996).

- On the visual forms of judicial theatre, and how they point towards the (imagined) source of law's authority, see Peter Goodrich, 'Visiocracy: On the Futures of the Fingerpost' (2013) 39 Critical Inquiry 498.

- For an exemplary analysis of a classically doctrinal debate in law (the debate between HLA Hart and Lon Fuller on the positive versus natural models of law), showing how the rhetorical form is linked to the substance of how we model law, see Desmond Manderson, 'HLA Hart, Lon Fuller and the Ghosts of Legal Interpretation' (2010) 28 Windsor Yearbook of Access to Justice 81.

- And on the rhetoric of William Blackstone's harmonious vision of the English common law, see Kathryn Temple, 'Sounds Couth and Uncouth: The Poetics of Harmonic Justice in William Blackstone's *Commentaries on the Laws of England*' (2015) 28 Law and Literature 97.

# 9 Creativity

Judgment is not a natural phenomenon. It does not spring forth automatically or from some perfect source of insight. It is something that is made. The activity of judges is, ultimately, a creative one: judges create judgments. Judgments, as nouns and verbs, are what judges make and do. The archive of preceding decisions upon which common law judges draw, similarly, were made and done—built or constructed by judges in the past. And this creation was and is done using a range of acknowledged and unacknowledged resources—many of which we have discussed across this book.

To resolve disputes, legal decisions must be made (Chapter 1) with authority (Chapter 2), with that authority seen, in part, to be found in the appropriate use of reason and logic (Chapter 3), and giving rise to itself as disciplinary truth (Chapter 4) and as a tool of governance (Chapter 5), which is also produced through performance and ritual (Chapter 6), involves ongoing practices of interpreting previous cases and texts (Chapter 7), and is underpinned by the rhetorical features of judicial practice and institution (Chapter 8). The multifaceted assemblage of judgment thus depends upon or is enabled by a whole range of things—from technologies of communication to the intellectual tools of reason, from historical records to theatrical performance.

In this brief concluding chapter, we will reflect on the broadly creative nature of judgment. Far from the opening assumptions of judgment as a simple activity, this chapter will depict judgment as an art form, as improvisation and creative expression. We will begin by unpacking the continuity that can be seen between the 'genres' of judgment and storytelling (section 9.1). The chapter will then examine the idea of judgment as a form of improvisation, in which judges inherently create the law through the process of judgment (section 9.2). The chapter—and the book—will then close with a short reflection on the over-arching artistic quality of judgment as a particular cultural form of expression, which this book has begun to set out some of the tools for unpacking (section 9.3).

DOI: 10.4324/9780429329784-9

## 9.1 Narrative

Judgments are stories. A provocative and potentially controversial statement, but one that bears some consideration. The premise here is that judgments—as written documents, as reasoned arguments—share many features with literary narrative. In academic research, this is often referred to by the phrase 'law as literature', and the basic premise is to apply the tools and insights of literary analysis to the 'genre' of text we call judgment—which we discussed in general in Chapter 7. This means examining and unpacking judgments in terms of their poetic or artistic qualities, their use of metaphor and structure, and the general form of judgment as a kind of writing. It recognises that there is a continuity between judgments and other forms of writing instead of assuming or holding that judgment is a distinct object that, in its objectivity and authority, is separated from the subjectivity and contingency of literary art.

In many ways, what this opens up to is a version of the question we were looking at in Chapters 2 and 3, and elsewhere—namely, how do we distinguish legal judgment (as authoritative) from other forms of opinion. But here, the question is asked on the level of the written form of judgment itself. There is much debate and analysis around this idea, but one model that is quite fruitful in understanding the literary form of judgment, specifically in terms of narrative (as well as the potential for literature to have a judicial function), is Jerome Bruner's *Making Stories*.[1]

In his short book, Bruner examines the general structure of storytelling. His basic argument is that all stories involve tension between what is expected to happen and what actually happens. Stories help us make sense of the disjunction between expectation and occurrence, which is why they typically involve some kind of rupture of normal life, some event that challenges what is expected by disrupting the usual order of things within the world of the story. So for example, aliens attack Manhattan, or Romeo and Juliette fall in love. And in any story, the narrative eventually resolves itself in one of two ways: either the 'old' normal is restored or a 'new' normal emerges. In either case, the process of the narrative works to deal with, manage, or otherwise resolve the disruption of normality—and thus stories and narratives are an important way in which we make sense of life.

Legal judgments, too, 'involve the subtle comparison of what was expected and what actually happened'.[2] In this general structure, then, can be seen a basic function of judgment as a legal decision from Chapter 1, as

---

1 Jemore Bruner, *Making Stories: Law, Literature, Life* (Harvard University Press 2002).
2 Bruner (n 1) 38.

the resolution of a harm or unwanted event. When something happens to disrupt the norms or values of a society, the legal institution processes that disruption and resolves it to an outcome. Like literature and storytelling, either things are put back where they were before the breach (e.g. the aliens are vanquished and Manhattan is safe, or damages are awarded to replace losses suffered due to a breach of contract) or a new normal is mandated in response to the harm (e.g. Romeo and Juliette suffer a tragic fate, or a criminal is imprisoned). In this way, Bruner claims that law has a literary structure and function: it operates on a narrative basis, resolving the unexpected disruptions to the normal order of social and communal life.

The rules and regulations of the state, the previous judgments of the common law, take their place amongst the other narratives of a culture and become the 'stock unexpected'[3] that are utilised and deployed to manage these disruptions. In quite a real sense, judgments tell stories about social life and normative values in order to make sense of what has happened and allow everyone to move on. As Bruner says, whether in law, literature, or life in general, narrative 'is our medium for coming to terms with the surprises and oddities of the human condition and for coming to terms with our imperfect grasp of that condition'.[4] Indeed, it can be said that it is narrative that gives us the ability to structure and understand the universe in general, as much as the normative orders of a culture, society, or legal system.

Our worlds generally are given structure by the narratives that provide their meanings. The idea of a world that is underpinned by norms or normative values can be labelled as a *nomos*: a normative order. This is a bigger idea than the prescriptions of the rules of law, encountering instead a more general notion of normativity and a culture's set of dominant social, ethical, and moral values. And as Robert Cover notes, a *nomos* is given meaning through narrative:

> History and literature cannot escape their location in a normative universe, nor can prescription, even when embodied in a legal text, escape its origin and its end in experience, in the narratives that are the trajectories plotted upon material reality by our imaginations.[5]

It is through storytelling, through the elaboration of narratives, that the ideas and conceptual structures and values of law and justice are given form. And this is so not only in the fables and myths that permeate cultural history, but

---

3 Bruner (n 1) 91.
4 Bruner (n 1) 90.
5 Robert Cover, 'Foreword: Nomos and Narrative' (1983) 97 Harvard Law Review 4, 5.

also in the narratives constructed through legal adjudication. As a narrative form, judgment takes its place on a continuum with other literary creations. Moreover, without its literary quality, law fails to be law:

> It is literature, writing in its most general sense and sensibility, inclusive of architectural, artistic, vestimentary and ceremonial, that inaugurates law in the social, as matter and as presence, tone and practice . . . .
> Law, in other words, without literary skill, imaginative expression and erudite interpretation . . . would simply sleep as an improbable attempt to terrorize the public sphere by means of a dictatorship of reason and a tyranny of rules.[6]

To be more than the assertion of logic (note the discussion in Chapter 3), to be something that is moral or just as opposed to simply an arbitrary rule, the judgments of law require literary skill in its broadest sense in order to undertake the rhetorical work examined in Chapter 8, as well as encountering the complex uncertainty of the moral and ethical questions raised by the cases that the courts must adjudicate.

To judge well requires wit and wisdom, the ability to work with complex texts and conceptual forms—not mere logic. But law does not collapse into other forms of literature. Judgment tends to appear in a form that we can read: law needs to circulate as a material object and be encountered through the senses—be it in a court transcript, a printed report, or a digital database, or the broader aesthetics of institutional theatre and architecture. The narratives told by judges as they mediate the vicissitudes of communal life, adjudicating between competing interests and values, thus take on a hermeneutic form—a form that mediates between its source and its audience.

Law's authoritative source, as explored in Chapter 2, is ultimately absent or invisible—it is the divine authority of the sovereign, or the infinite history of the common law, or (more mundanely) a reported decision that cannot be fully reproduced in the current judgment, or a judicial decision that is not fully 'captured' in its written report. The common law is not codified, not set down in advance, and thus, its judgments seek to communicate that which is unwritten. And this means, for Goodrich at least, that imaginary things gain the status of law: 'invisible entities, ghosts and other images, spectres and further inventions can emerge more easily, can gain dogmatic status, doctrinal recognition, become part of . . . the common law'.[7] And it is these 'dogmatic' concepts and imaginary things—the things that are not

---

6  Peter Goodrich, *Advanced Introduction to Law and Literature* (Edward Elgar 2021) 16–17.
7  Goodrich (n 6) 32.

present in the current decision but that are cited or otherwise pointed to and that exist 'before' or 'behind' judgment—that control and delimit its narrative scope and interpretive practices.

Judicial narrative, then, is something constructed and built as a broadly literary activity—but it is not created out of nothing, as if judges make it up as they go along. The meanings of texts and the available doctrines and interpretations of the common law exist in imaginary or materially absent form—as ideas, concepts, precepts, assumptions, ideology, convention. These 'unseen' dimensions of the law are then divined or made manifest through the material assemblage of judgment, encompassing not only the written form but also the spoken and theatrical performance of the court, as well as, potentially, the wider theatre of society and politics (see Chapter 6). Nevertheless, the question of the creativity of judgment—of the somewhat improvised nature of judgment that sits in tension with the assumed ideal that judges follow the law that is already laid down in the past—requires more direct attention, and this is the task of the next section.

## 9.2 Improvisation

The law exists independent of judicial discretion and constrains that discretion. Judges making decisions are bound by the law, which comes from elsewhere—be it the authority of the legislature or the immemorial past of the common law. Or so some understandings of judgment might have you believe. Indeed, judges themselves often invoke this principle—that they are merely the passive mouthpieces of the law, which ultimately stems from elsewhere. Usually, this 'elsewhere' is located in parliament—and courts will wash their hands of certain problematic areas of doctrine by claiming only parliament can actually change the law. And judges sometimes say this even in the context of purely common law doctrine, which is not (yet) codified by statute. And so goes the separation of powers: legislature creates law, judiciary interprets and applies it, and executive directs and enforces it. Thus, common law judgment operates to mediate the principles of statutory law as it does those of the common law itself, but not to change it (see Chapter 1).

Yet there are equally many examples where the courts actually do change or create the law. Framed in the guise of interpretation (see Chapter 7), there is a very real sense in which judgment creates or amends the law in most, if not all cases: by determining what the words of the law mean (be they statutory or found in the archive of recorded decisions), judgment determines what the law is and can thus be said to create it through that interpretive act. Judgment is not (wholly) bound by rules or doctrines coming from elsewhere but is (also) constructed by judges themselves. Judgments are created, constructed from legal materials—not given to judges in advance (whether they are determining a case in the supreme court or a problem scenario in an exam hall).

Yet this idea of judicial improvisation seems to contradict the key premise of the authority of law, that it is set in advance and applied impartially through an objective process. If law is made up as we go along, then how is that fair and impartial? How is that justice? The previous section has already begun to indicate an aspect of this, in terms of the way judgments operate as part of the narrative functions of culture to 'manage' deviations from what was expected to happen. In this way, the rules of law become pre-set narratives that are drawn upon in the making of a judgment—telling a new narrative—to process and move past the rupture to our social, communal, or normative order.

The process of judgment itself—the decision in the present case—is not known in advance; it has not yet been narrated by the legal institution. It is only by rendering judgment—by writing the story, as it were—that this is done and the law is applied to the facts and thus becomes known. Importantly, this is not done in a vacuum: the improvisational quality of judgment in this sense is not simply judges making it up as they go along—but is instead judges drawing on a rich history, tradition, and set of conventions, expertise, and expectations around how certain kinds of situations, facts, and events should be categorised and dealt with in light of the legal resources available.

But the improvisational quality of judgment runs deeper than this once we recognise, more critically, what improvisation actually entails. Indeed, it can be observed that true improvisation—*actually* making it up as you go along—is impossible. Decisions, actions, interpretations, and meanings are always constrained in some way by what has gone before. And improvisation actually relies upon preceding structures and resources in order to work—even jazz, as Sara Ramshaw tells us at intricate length, has a whole complex set of rules and conventions that shape its supposedly 'free' and 'wild' musical forms, and that jazz musicians draw and build upon when they play: 'Improvisation requires . . . a comprehensive knowledge of the *tradition*' that someone is working within.[8]

Indeed, it also relies upon the repetition of existing things. We have noted a few times now how the material expression or writing of law is required in order for it to be communicated and read and, therefore, to regulate society. The same is true for everything else: for an improvised performance to be legible, for it to make some kind of sense or have any meaning at all, it must

---

8  Sara Ramshaw, *Justice as Improvisation: The Law of the Extempore* (Routledge 2013) 79.

utilise existing resources for making-meaning, such as certain conventions in musical structure (notes, scales, time signatures) or, for example, words, signs, and symbols. That is, it must repeat things that have gone before. Repetition is necessary for improvisation. But paradoxically, it is by improvising that the law can adapt to new and specific cases and events—that the rules of the past can be interpreted, updated, and applied to life. Ramshaw again:

> improvisation both affirms the law as it is and as it can be otherwise. The glance towards infinite possibility impedes closure and enables change and transformation within a given system. Novelty enters through repetition, which is simultaneously same and other.[9]

Applying improvisation to law, the potential for infinite variation that it may seem to open up actually enables otherwise rigid rules to be applied to instant cases. Judgment 'glances' towards the infinite potential for interpretation (see Chapter 7), enabling innovation and creativity within judicial processes that can help 'solve' the problem before the court. The innovation of judgment is both new and novel, as well as a repetition of the previously established law: it is both 'the same' law (so it can be legible and understood) and an 'other' law invented in the current case (so it can deal with the specifics of the current case). The new inscription of the law in each case updates and translates the previous law into the present. 'The verdict is not simply the truth as found and spoken by jury or fact finder, it is also, at the level of doctrine, the . . . new meaning that the judgment inscribes into law.'[10]

## 9.3 Expression

Judgments do more than simply resolve individual disputes or build up into relatively stable bodies of doctrine. They also mediate general principles with specific cases, continuing to narrate and improvise the answers to moral, ethical, and social questions as new cases arise. In doing this, they encounter a range of complexities—some of which this book has touched upon or briefly indicated. But they also say something. Not just about specific cases or how we might interpret doctrine, but about the values and ideals of a society, a community, and an individual.

We have noted previously in this book's journey how judgments may embed (unconscious) factors of the judge's own preferences and reasons

---

9 Ramshaw (n 8) 128.
10 Goodrich (n 6) 65.

for decision, which we might unpack through certain kinds of reading. But once we acknowledge that the creative nature of judgment runs closer to the surface than this, once we see that the common law method (of applying bodies of principle to novel cases in order to resolve their specific disputes, as much as the challenge they represent for the order of society and the integrity of the common law) is one that is necessarily predicated upon improvisation, then the expressive nature of judgment becomes even more readily apparent.

It is in these moments of uncertainty, where an event raises a question for the law and the institution of judgment orients its resources and methods and assumptions towards it, that something is revealed. The way judgments are resolved, the way decisions are made, the kinds of methods and approaches that are accepted as legitimate: all these things reveal the values and ideals of a community, or at least of the certain sections of a community involved in its production and validation. Judgments are symptomatic of the structures and assumptions that shape and underpin the law and its institution. By reading judgments carefully, by orienting a wide range of methods and perspectives (some of which this book has indicated) to understanding, unpacking, and analysing judicial forms and outcomes, we can begin to understand some of these aspects and gain a fuller appreciation for the complexities and significance of common law processes within and beyond the internal dimensions of legal doctrine.

Judgment is an art form, a creative practice steeped in tradition and convention like any other artistic practice—conventions like *stare decisis* (Chapter 1), reason (Chapter 3), written language (Chapter 5), ritual (Chapter 6), or the limitation of meaning (Chapter 7). And in studying this art, in reading and examining it through a wide variety of lenses, with variable and unsettled assumptions, we may come to detect what it might tell us about ourselves—as communal beings, as humans, as entities betrothed to institutional forms.

It is hoped that this book has provided its reader with a number of different, and perhaps conflicting, trajectories that can be followed when engaging with legal judgment and what it might express. The intent is that a range of methods have been travelled through the reading of this book, a range that does not prioritise any particular approach or pretend that any single one is sealed off or independent from any other. All being well, the various sections and chapters of this book will serve as something like a database or collection of different ways of understanding what judges do, produce, or bring about, and a collection that does not shy away from the complexities of the intellectual and cultural associations or baggage that comes with developing that understanding. And perhaps most importantly, this book has aimed to demonstrate that the work of judgment is something to be questioned, in multifarious ways, and is something that is never clear, never certain or given in advance—and never complete.

## 9.4 Further reading

- For a fuller discussion on the use of narrative in order to make sense of life, including in law, see Jerome Bruner, *Making Stories: Law, Literature, Life* (Harvard University Press 2002).
- On the concept of *nomos* or normative universe, and the way it is established and maintained through narrative, see Robert Cover, 'Foreword: Nomos and Narrative' (1983) 97 Harvard Law Review 4.
- Also listed in Chapter 7, Peter Goodrich, *Advanced Introduction to Law and Literature* (Edward Elgar 2021) is worth repeating here as an extended introduction to the creative genre of judicial writing or 'jurisliterature'.
- For an extended and advanced discussion of the way extraordinary cases break away from assumed norms and enable law to evolve and produce new norms (as well as the rich connections between the expressive genres of art and law), see Angela Condello, 'Between Ordinary and Extraordinary: The Normativity of the Singular Case in Art and Law' (2018) 2 Art and Law 1.
- For an analysis of the famous English case of *R v R* (which abolished the marital exception for the offence of rape) using the work of Derrida, and ideas around the invented, performative, and fictional qualities of law, see Chris Lloyd, ' "*Ce Qui Arrive*": Deconstruction, Invention and the Legal Subject of *R v R*' (2012) 37 Australian Feminist Law Journal 65.
- But for a full examination of the improvisational nature of judgment (taking many lessons from the structure of jazz improvisation), one cannot go wrong by consulting Sara Ramshaw, *Justice as Improvisation: The Law of the Extempore* (Routledge 2013). For a shorter outline of Ramshaw's key ideas, see Sara Ramshaw, 'The Paradox of Performative Immediacy: Law, Music, Improvisation' (2016) 12 Law, Culture and the Humanities 6.

# Index

Printed in the United States
by Baker & Taylor Publisher Services